Better Homes and Gardens.

Favorite American Wines
& How to Enjoy Them

© 1979 by Meredith Corporation, Des Moines, Iowa.
All Rights Reserved. Printed in the United States of America.
First Edition. First Printing.
Library of Congress Catalog Card Number: 78-73185
ISBN: 0-696-00385-6

BETTER HOMES AND GARDENS® BOOKS

Editor-in-Chief: James A. Autry
Editorial Director: Neil Kuehnl
Executive Art Director: William J. Yates

Editor: Gerald M. Knox
Art Director: Ernest Shelton
Associate Art Director: Randall Yontz
Copy and Production Editors: David Kirchner,
David A. Walsh
Senior Graphic Designer: Harijs Priekulis
Graphic Designers: Sheryl Veenschoten,
Richard Lewis, Neoma Alt West, Linda Ford,
Tom Wegner

Food Editor: Doris Eby
Senior Associate Food Editor: Sharyl Heiken
Senior Food Editors: Sandra Granseth,
Elizabeth Woolever
Associate Food Editors: Diane Nelson,
Joy L. Taylor, Patricia Teberg
Recipe Development Editor: Marion Viall

Favorite American Wines and How to Enjoy Them
Our special thanks to Better Homes and Gardens'
Contributing Wine Editor: Ruth Ellen Church

Copy and Production Editor: Paul S. Kitzke
Graphic Designer: Faith Berven
Wine-making photographs: Fred Lyon, Ozzie Sweet,
David Jordan

Contents

Better Homes and Gardens
TEST KITCHEN ®

Our seal assures you that every recipe in *Favorite American Wines* is endorsed by the Better Homes and Gardens Test Kitchen. Each recipe is tested for family appeal, practicality, and deliciousness.

Wine Prices: The prices listed in this book are for the new 750-milliliter bottle (close to the old "fifth" in size), unless otherwise stated. Prices do vary from state to state, and are subject to change.

Welcome to Wine

This is not a book for wine experts—they have libraries of their own already. Our new *Better Homes and Gardens* guide to American wines is for people like you who want to enjoy serving and sipping wines—and using

them in your kitchen as well. We've organized it to help you find what you need quickly. Our A-to-Z chapter (pages 8 to 45) briefly describes more than 50 American wines, so you can feel more knowledgeable both at home and in a wine shop. The section on how wine is made (pages 46 to 61) is based on step-by-step photographs, rather than on complex technical details. Our serving information (pages 62 to 71) is aimed at simplifying, not complicating. Recipes using wine (pages 72-91) were chosen from the vast *Better Homes and Gardens* collection of tested recipes. So use this book with confidence—and remember that above all, wine is to enjoy.

Understanding American Wines

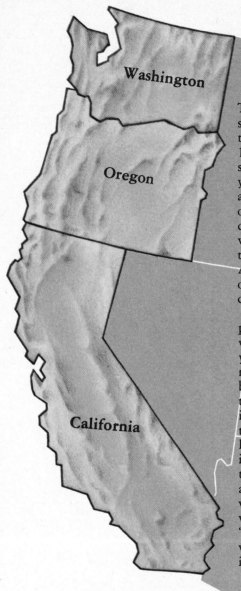

The American wine industry started virtually from zero after the repeal of Prohibition in 1933. Compare the few decades since then to the hundreds of years in which French, German, and Italian wines have developed, and it's a wonder that we can enjoy so many top-notch wines. Indeed, in blind (unidentified) tasting sessions, many American wines have equaled or surpassed famous European counterparts.

California, of course, is our premier grape-growing and wine-making state. In the first years after Prohibition, California vintners produced mostly blended, bulk wines with a bias toward sweetness. But as Americans began drinking more wine, they also learned to enjoy lighter, drier wines with more individuality. Thus began a shift toward *varietal* wines named after the grapes from which they were made—rather than *generic* wines such as "burgundy," "chablis," "port," and "sherry," with names that mean very little in this country.

The majority of wines listed in this book are varietals. California varietal wines include Cabernet Sauvignon (our best red wine), Chardonnay (our best white), Chenin Blanc, Zinfandel, and even the tongue-twisting Gewürztraminer. Some of these and other varietal wines are also being produced in the Pacific Northwest, the Midwest, East, and parts of the South.

In addition, the wine listings in this book include new *hybrid* varietals, which are less familiar to most Americans. They are crosses between various kinds of grapes—usually in an attempt to breed more hardiness and productivity into the vines. Examples of such hybrids include Aurora, Baco Noir, and Seyval Blanc. They are revolutionizing wine making, especially in the Midwest and East, and you'll enjoy tasting them.

This map gives you a quick overview of this country's most active wine-making states (in green). In our A-to-Z chapter, specific wineries are listed in each state for each type of wine.

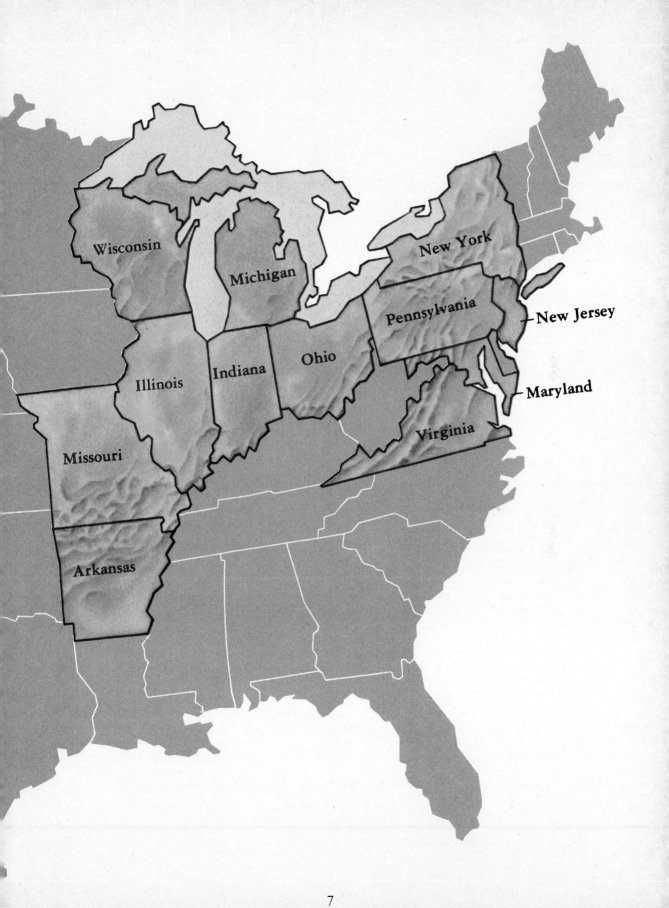

Wisconsin

Michigan

New York

Pennsylvania

New Jersey

Illinois

Indiana

Ohio

Maryland

Missouri

Virginia

Arkansas

How to Look Up a Wine

The next chapter, pages 10 to 45, lists more than 50 American wines alphabetically. It provides basic information about each wine's origins, how it tastes, what to serve with it, the price range for it (in the new 750-milliliter bottle), who makes it, and—in many cases—special tips on drinking or using it.

But before going to that chapter, practice a bit on wine labels right here. Information on wine labels is by no means standardized. This first column shows a relatively easy label. Widmer is the name of the winery, and the type of wine is *port* —so look under "P" in the next chapter.

"Special Selection" may or may not tell anything about the wine's quality (the law is vague on such points), but "New York State" certainly describes where it came from. "Cuvée," a French word for "vatful," signifies a particular numbered batch of wine made by this winery.

Other lines give serving suggestions, the winery's exact location, and the alcoholic content. Most table (dinner) wines are in the 11 to 13 percent alcohol range; the heavier dessert wines, such as port, are usually fortified with brandy and have alcohol contents of between 17 and 20 percent.

Now try a somewhat more complicated label. "Solera" indicates that the wine was made by the Spanish *solera* system of blending in stacked casks (see page 42). (Even if you don't know what "Solera" means, the word's placement away from the center of the label suggests it isn't the name of the wine.) Sebastiani is the winery that produced it in Northern California. Cream Sherry is one type of *sherry*—listed under "S" in the next chapter. *Amore* is the Italian word for love. "Full-Bodied and Sweet" is the winemaker's description of the kind of product he's placed in this bottle. Finally, as before, come the winery's location and the wine's alcohol content.

Many wine labels have still other important-looking words on them. Some you'll find in the "Glossary of Wine Terms" on page 93. But sometimes you will need to spot which word is actually the name of the wine. It will probably be listed in the A-to-Z chapter that follows.

Here's a deceptively simple wine label. The winery clearly is Charles Krug, and the wine—which is produced in the famous Napa Valley of Northern California—appears to be named Pinot Chardonnay.

However, you won't find it under "P" in this book. It's under "C" for Chardonnay, which is the name gradually being agreed upon by most wineries and wine experts. As you'll see in the listing itself, the "Pinot" is technically incorrect based on the French heritage of this varietal grape.

Similarly, many American wines made from the same grape appear under a variety of names. The index (pages 95 and 96) cross-references many of them, so if you don't find what you are looking for in the A-to-Z chapter, check the index to see whether your wine has a different preferred name.

Because Chardonnay is a dry table wine, its alcohol content falls within the 11 to 13 percent range. Incidentally, small differences of a percent or so in alcohol between two wines of the same type have little bearing on either the quality or the taste of what you pour into your glass.

Occasionally you'll come across a label like this one—where the name of the wine is *proprietary* and belongs exclusively to one winery. "Beaurosé" combines the name of Beaulieu Vineyard with the *generic* (common) name rosé, the French word for pink. This book doesn't list all such cases; here, fortunately, the producer indicates what the wine is: "a light rosé." That last name is listed under "R" in the A-to-Z chapter.

Remember, too, that the back label on a wine bottle (if it has one) provides additional information on the product within. Sometimes the specific grapes are described; more commonly, the vintner indicates the wine's dryness or sweetness, along with serving suggestions and facts relating to making it.

Aurora (or Aurore)

(a-ROAR-a, oh-ROAR)

Both the French and American spellings and pronunciations are used for this relatively new addition to our wine lists. Made from excellent French-American hybrid grapes, this white wine is coming into its own east of the Mississippi, especially in Michigan and New York. The vines are fairly prolific. Their pale yellow grapes turn a spectacular pink at harvesttime. An early September harvest is a distinct advantage in the East, where winter comes early. Vineyard acreage is expanding; Aurora has become a standard wine in the East, useful also in blends with other wines, and as a base for sparkling wines.

How it tastes: Usually semisweet, though a few wineries ferment it dry. Rather neutral in taste to begin with, Aurora takes on a distinct aroma and flavor when aged in oak. It reminds some wine drinkers of a cross between American chablis and sauterne.

How to serve: A dry Aurora may be served with fish and seafood, but the more usual semisweet wine is better suited to light luncheon dishes, such as ham prepared with fruit.

Price: $3.50 to $5.

Who makes Aurora: New York: Benmarl, Bully Hill, Great Western, Johnson Estate. Michigan: Bronte, Fenn Valley, Warner. Wisconsin: Wollersheim.

Special note: Drink Aurora wine about three years old for best flavor. If quality is exceptional, it will keep eight to ten years in cool storage.

Baco Noir

(BAH-ko NWAHR)

Blue-black, early-ripening, French-American hybrid grapes make this full-bodied, deep red wine. Grown extensively in the Eastern United States, these vines are valued for their vigor and hardiness in cold winters, as well as the fine quality of Baco Noir wine, one of our two most popular dry table wines made from new hybrid grapes (Seyval Blanc is the other). Of Cabernet Sauvignon descent, Baco grapes produce wine that ages well.

How it tastes: A little harsh when young, Baco mellows in time. The better wineries age it in casks for several years, after which it often resembles a good California Cabernet Sauvignon or French Bordeaux wine.

How to serve: Serve a mature Baco Noir with roast beef, pot roast, stew, or steak, or with lamb, duck, or game. It complements many kinds of cheese, including the fine cheddars of New York and Wisconsin, as well as blue cheese.

Price: $3 to $4.50 or more.

Who makes Baco Noir: Arkansas: Wiederkehr. Indiana: Easley's Cape Sandy, Oliver, Villa Medeo. Michigan: Bronte, Fenn Valley, Tabor Hill, Warner. Missouri: Bardenheier's, St. James. New York: Benmarl, Bully Hill, Great Western, Villa D'Ingianni. Ohio: Warren Sublette, Valley Vineyards. Pennsylvania: Mazza, Penn Shore. Wisconsin: Wollersheim.

Special note: The ambitious Baco Noir vines grow fast and make an attractive grape arbor.

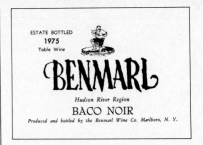

Barbera

(Bar-BEAR-a)

A northern Italian grape that in California makes a robust, deep red, Italian-style wine—especially when grown in the cooler coastal counties. Popularized by Italian winemakers, such as Louis M. Martini and August Sebastiani, Barbera now is made by at least three dozen California wineries in a wide price range. In general, you get the quality you pay for; the inexpensive Barberas are very drinkable, though they aren't aged in oak for long life as are the expensive ones. Barbera is rapidly replacing so-called American "chianti" wine, because the latter term is essentially meaningless here and can refer to any Italian-style red wine.

VINEYARDS ESTABLISHED 1825

1970

Sebastiani

FOUNDED AT THE END OF EL CAMINO REAL

NORTH COAST COUNTIES

BARBERA

Bold and Robust

PRODUCED AND BOTTLED BY SEBASTIANI VINEYARDS

SONOMA VALLEY, CALIFORNIA

ALC. 12½% BY VOL. BONDED WINERY 876

How it tastes: Fresh, quite tart and fruity. If aged, it's very mellow but will still pucker your taste buds. Barbera is one of our best wines for bringing out and enhancing the flavor of foods.

How to serve: The young, inexpensive Barberas stand up well to highly seasoned, even garlicky Italian dishes; the aged, more expensive Barberas are well suited to beef, game, and flavorful cheeses, including blue, Roquefort, Stilton, and Gorgonzola.

Price: $2 from the volume producers; $3 to $4 for excellent quality; up to $6 or $7 for long-lived Barberas.

Who makes Barbera: Almadén, Bargetto, Buena Vista, California Growers, Gallo, Heitz, Inglenook, M. La Mont, Louis M. Martini, Paul Masson, Sebastiani, Winemaster's Guild, others.

Special note: You may want to compare California's Barbera with Italy's; look for Barbera d' Alba or Barbera d' Asti.

Burgundy

(BUR-gun-dy)

Burgundy in the United States is a generic term for any blended red table wine. In the Burgundy district of France, Burgundy is either red wine made of Pinot Noir grapes or white wine made of Chardonnay grapes. There is no relationship between an American "burgundy" and a true French Burgundy, because Pinot Noir and Chardonnay are expensive grapes, and they are not used to make the inexpensive burgundy wines of the United States.

To avoid using the imitative "burgundy" name (which, however, is perfectly legal here), many wineries have switched to other names— sometimes simply "Such-and-Such Winery Red (or Mountain Red) Wine." Sparkling burgundy is also available; it is less expensive than champagne but usually rather sweet (see page 60).

There are plenty of good, drinkable, inexpensive wines calling themselves burgundy— from all parts of the country, not just from California. Taste several. When you find one you especially like, buy it by the "jug"—such as the new metric 1.5-liter size. In many states, burgundy is available in large three-liter bottles, too.

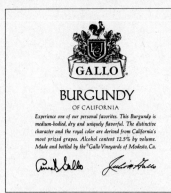

How it tastes: Usually dry, mellow, and soft, to appeal to a mass market. But because many different grapes are used, many different tastes (even a few sweet ones) are found in wines called burgundy. If you like red wine, try several different burgundies from various wineries until you settle on a favorite or two.

How to serve: This is everyday wine to serve at a cool room temperature with a variety of everyday foods—hamburgers, ham-and-cheese sandwiches, ground beef casseroles, spaghetti and meatballs, fried chicken, barbecued ribs, picnic fare.

Price: Around $2 for 750 milliliters; $3 to $4 is typical for 1.5 liters. However, both price and quality vary more than with most other American wines.

Who makes U.S. "burgundy": Hundreds of wineries do. The following can generally be relied upon to furnish good wine at a fair price. California: Almadén, Christian Brothers, Cresta Blanca, Franzia, Gallo, Inglenook, Italian Swiss Colony, M. La Mont, Louis M. Martini, Paul Masson, Parducci, San Martín, Sebastiani, Weibel. New York: Gold Seal, Great Western, Taylor.

Special note: If you buy large bottles of burgundy but worry about the wine spoiling before you have time to drink it all, here's a tip: Re-bottle the wine in clean small bottles, corking them well. A three-liter jug will give you four 750-milliliter portions. Keep the bottles refrigerated, and use them at a reasonable rate.

Cabernet Sauvignon

(Kab-er-nay SO-veen-yon)

This great red wine grape of Bordeaux, France, is responsible for the high quality of some of the world's most celebrated wines—the most coveted vintages of famous chateaux (large French estates where wine is made). They are wines that may last a hundred years; a single ancient bottle of such wine may sell for thousands of dollars. Even the newest wines from these French chateaux are quite expensive.

In California's cool coastal regions, Cabernet Sauvignon vines produce grapes for wines so fine they have established a very respected place for California (and the United States) in the wine

world. The vines are difficult to grow, and they bear fruit sparingly. As a result, this garnet-colored wine is costly to produce.

Even in the harsher climate of our Eastern states, growers and producers are planting Cabernet Sauvignon vines in an attempt to prove that fine wines are not exclusively French or Californian. Only time will tell of their success or failure.

How it tastes: Carefully aged Cabernet Sauvignon offers a complexity of bouquet and flavors that delights and inspires. A deep, rich wine, it tastes of berries, herbs, even mint. On the other hand, a young Cabernet—particularly one that will someday, after aging in the bottle, be velvety smooth—can be rather harsh and leave a bitter taste in the back of the mouth. So you'll want to sample a Cabernet Sauvignon from several vintage years and in several price ranges before deciding on one that's a particularly good value.

How to serve: A lot of ritual surrounds the serving of a California Cabernet Sauvignon of superior quality. But not all Cabernet is that good. A bottle eight to ten years old from a respected winemaker deserves respect and should accompany a succulent roast or other special meat. Much Cabernet Sauvignon is less than four or five years old, however, and it may not have any special pedigree. So uncork it, pour, and serve with whatever's for dinner—

provided the dish is not too spicy. Beef, lamb, pork, roast turkey, duck, or even a good casserole of meat and potatoes may be enhanced by a welcome bottle of Cabernet Sauvignon.

Price: $3.50 to $5 for an average but not exceptional bottle; as much as $25 for a prestigious one from an outstanding vintage year and a fine winery.

Who makes Cabernet Sauvignon: Many (about 150) California wineries make it—the coastal locations with the greatest success. You might start with the Christian Brothers, which blends several vintage years rather than dating the bottles. A few wineries are now making interesting rosé wines from Cabernet Sauvignon grapes: Buena Vista, Dry Creek, Firestone, Geyser Peak, Llords & Elwood, Simi, Sterling, others.

Special note: Cabernet Sauvignon is America's finest red wine, with great competition for the vintage bottles from certain small but famous Napa Valley wineries—so much so that prices tend to get out of hand. Keep in mind that even the most highly praised wines can occasionally prove an expensive disappointment, and that a selection of several modestly priced Cabernet Sauvignons may offer more pleasure to you than a single overpriced bottle.

Carignane

(CARE-ee-nyon; incorrectly pronounced "Kerrigan")

A red wine grape grown extensively in Spain and southern France as well as in California. The vines are highly productive, so this wine has long been used in "burgundy" blends and to help stretch the wine yield from scarcer grapes. Now, however, Carignane has been rediscovered as a very drinkable wine. With no distinctive flavor of its own, it is sometimes made more interesting by the addition of some Merlot wine.

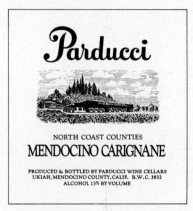

Parducci

NORTH COAST COUNTIES
MENDOCINO CARIGNANE

PRODUCED & BOTTLED BY PARDUCCI WINE CELLARS
UKIAH, MENDOCINO COUNTY, CALIF. B.W.C. 3832
ALCOHOL 13% BY VOLUME

How it tastes: Most of it is dry, a bit fruity. Carignane is a good choice when you want to advance from ordinary "burgundy" to a true varietal wine.

How to serve: Cool or lightly chilled, with everyday foods—a ham sandwich; spaghetti; Spanish rice; a mushroom, green pepper, and tomato omelet.

Price: From $2.50 to $3.50.

Who makes Carignane: California Growers, Fetzer, Heitz, Papagni, Parducci, Simi, Trentadue, half a dozen others.

Special note: Carignane is a good base for *sangria*, the fruited wine punch from Spain. Pour wine into a pitcher, add thin slices of lemon and orange, then sparkling water.

Catawba

(Kuh-TAW-buh)

Purplish-red, native Eastern grapes and their red, white, or pink wine. Prolific winter-hardy Catawba grapes are used to make sparkling wines as well as still wines.

How it tastes: Sweet, in varying degrees, with a strong, grapy flavor and aroma.
How to serve: Well chilled by itself or as a dessert wine. Pour it over fresh fruits.
Price: $1.75 to $2.25.
Who makes Catawba: About 40 wineries, including: Arkansas: Post's Winery. Illinois: Mogen David. Michigan: Bronte. Missouri: Bardenheier's. New York: Barry, Canandaigua, Gold Seal, Taylor, Widmer's. Ohio: Catawba Island, Meier's, Warren J. Sublette, Valley Vineyards.

Chablis

(Shahb-LEE)

Generic term for an inexpensive, everyday white wine, the U.S. companion to everyday red "burgundy." Although it can be very good, it should not be confused with true French Chablis, which is a white Burgundy wine made from Chardonnay grapes—an aristocrat at the dining table.
American chablis is a blend of various white grape varieties, but Chardonnay seldom enters that blend because it is too expensive. French Colombard and Chenin Blanc may be included in the blend for a California chablis, while there might be some Delaware and Seyval Blanc in an Eastern chablis. Each winery develops its own formula for chablis, depending on the available inexpensive grapes. Overall, the U.S. quality is surprisingly good. Though our white wines called chablis are undistinguished, they are almost always pleasant—as well as kind to your budget.
There is a small but hopeful trend toward dropping this borrowed name in this country. Though perfectly legal in America, our "chablis" and "burgundy" are regarded as deceptive labels in Europe. So some wineries have switched to "Mountain White," "Vineyard White," or simply "White Table Wine" preceded by the name of the winery.

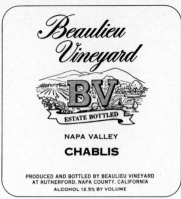

How it tastes: Good U.S. chablis is a dry, fresh, fruity white wine—but beyond that, there is a wide choice but little consistency from winery to winery. Nearly all our chablis is pleasant in one way or another, depending on how you like your white wine to taste. Sampling several versions from different producers is the best way to find one you particularly like.
How to serve: Well chilled, as an appetizer wine; with simple foods—a tuna salad, a chicken sandwich, frankfurters, corned beef hash, creamed or fried fish.
Price: Around $2. In many states, chablis is also available in proportionately less expensive 1.5- and three-liter bottles.
Who makes U.S. "chablis": Most wineries—but some, as mentioned, now employ other names for their basic white wines. Gallo makes a particularly good Chablis Blanc at an especially attractive price. Other popular choices include Almadén, Beaulieu, CK, Christian Brothers, Inglenook, Paul Masson, Mirassou. In New York: Great Western.
Special note: When you find a chablis that you enjoy drinking, buy it by the jug and cook with it, too.

Champagne

(Sham-PAIN)

Here's another case where an originally meaningful French word has come to America and become a generic, all-inclusive name for sparkling, effervescent white wines. (The French have not been overjoyed by this.) Most U.S. champagnes are white, although there are a few pink varieties, and sparkling bur-

gundy (red) and cold duck (various colors) are also available. The bubbles come from a secondary (later) fermentation—either in the bottle itself or through a newer, bulk process. See page 60 for details on how champagne is made.

How it tastes: A freshly opened bottle of champagne is so fizzy that many people forget to react to its aroma and flavor. There's quite a difference from one champagne to another—depending on what grapes are used and how dry it is made. The driest ones are labeled "brut" and the somewhat sweeter champagnes are called "extra dry" (confusing, but that's the way it is). Still sweeter champagnes are labeled "sec."

For serving information, turn the page.

How to serve: Champagne typically replaces cocktails at festive occasions—weddings or family celebrations, for example. Serve it very cold, and open the bottle very gently with a towel over the cork so it can't rocket across the room. (As with a soft drink, avoid shaking the bottle so it won't overflow when you remove the cork.) And remember to make a glowing toast to a friend, a loved one, or to long life and happiness for all.

Price: $4 to $10.

Who makes champagne: A wide variety of California wineries, plus some well-known New York state wineries. California: Krug, Korbel, Kornell, Mirassou, Weibel, Christian Brothers, Paul Masson, Sonoma, Schramsberg, Almadén. New York: Gold Seal, Taylor, Great Western.

Special note: Champagne does not improve in the bottle; in fact, it eventually deteriorates. So if you receive a gift bottle, don't put it away for a far-off special occasion. Drink it soon —and enjoy!

Charbono

(Shar-bo-no)

For years, this robust red wine was made only by Inglenook in this country, as a house specialty. Recently, however, other California wineries have begun bottling it; its popularity is growing.

There's some disagreement as to whether the original Charbono grapes came from the Piedmont district in Italy or from what now is the Savoy district in France. In any case, today's California winemasters are producing an Italian-style wine to go with the Italian name it carries.

NAPA VALLEY
CHARBONO

Full bodied dry deep red table wine characteristic aroma and rich robust flavor **1971** *of our famed Charbono grape grown in Napa Valley. Serve at cool room temperature. Produced and Bottled by Inglenook Vineyards Rutherford, California. Alcohol 12% by Volume.*

How it tastes: Quite pungent in flavor, Charbono also has unexpected body. It's tart and dry—similar to Barbera but, if aged, perhaps softer on your palate. Tannin in the young wine may pucker your mouth a bit. Aging smooths it out.

How to serve: Try Charbono with pasta, of course, but also with hamburgers, roasts, hearty meats, or casseroles of all kinds.

Price: In the $3.50 to $5 range.

Who makes Charbono: Inglenook is still the prime producer, but Davis Bynum, Franciscan Vineyards, Angelo Papagni, Parducci, and Souverain also offer good versions.

Chardonnay (or Pinot Chardonnay)

(PEA-no SHAR-don-nay)

More and more wineries are dropping the word "pinot," which is actually incorrect because it isn't in the pinot family, as once thought. A noble white wine from the grape of the great white French Burgundies and Champagnes, Chardonnay makes magnificent but costly wine in California, especially in Napa Valley. With special care, the grapes can be grown in the Finger Lakes district of New York and a few scattered, protected areas in the East and Midwest. Washington State also grows Chardonnay. More than with most wines, the quality depends on each year's precise growing conditions, as well as the skill with which the wine is made.

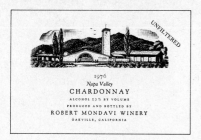

How it tastes: At its best, the pale, straw-colored wine (sometimes with a hint of green) has a restrained peach or apple flavor. It can be fresh and fruity when not aged in oak casks. Most of our expensive Chardonnays *are* aged, however, to give the wine character and bring out its subtleties of aroma and taste.

How to serve: With oysters, lobsters, other seafood, sole, trout, and other fine fish; with veal, turkey, special chicken recipes. Chardonnay is a fine wine for fine food.

Inexperienced wine drinkers often think Chardonnay is overpriced, because to them it is just another "nice white wine." That's why chablis or Chenin Blanc are better choices for such beginning palates. The complex, delightful flavors of a fine Chardonnay deserve to be savored and enjoyed at leisure —either as a pre-dinner or dinner wine.

Price: $3 to $10 or more (it is an expensive wine to make).

Who makes Chardonnay: Almost every winery in a suitably cool climate tries for this temperamental jewel. At a modest price (under $4), Paul Masson makes a good one.

Most of the successful Chardonnays are products of small Napa, Sonoma, or Monterey County wineries in California. In the middle price range, $5 to $7, try any of these: Charles Krug, Mirassou, Robert Mondavi, Monterey Vineyard, Sonoma Vineyards, Pedroncelli, Souverain, Wente. Recommended also from New York State: Gold Seal, Konstantin Frank. Michigan: Tabor Hill. Pennsylvania: Presque Isle. Washington: Ste. Michelle.

Special note: Very good Chardonnay will keep and improve in a cool wine cellar for six to eight years after bottling. This is unusual for a white wine; most whites should be consumed while young.

Chelois

(SHELL-wah, or sometimes Americanized to Shell-OY)

French-American hybrid grapes that have become a standard in Midwestern and Eastern vineyards, and the crimson wine they make. Chelois improves considerably with age, somewhat resembling a true Burgundy.

How it tastes: Somewhat harsh when young, this robust wine softens and mellows in oak casks and in the bottle.

How to serve: With roasts, pot roasts, game, Italian dishes, sausage, or cheese.

Price: Around $3.

Who makes Chelois: Indiana: Easley's, Oliver. Kentucky: Colcord. Michigan: Warner. Missouri: Bardenheier's, Green Valley, Stoltz, Stone Mill. New York: Benmarl, Great Western. Other vineyards in Ohio, Pennsylvania, Wisconsin.

Chenin Blanc

(SHEN-in BLAWN)

The grapes originated in the Loire Valley of France; the wine, one of California's most delightful, currently enjoys great popularity. It's a logical step upward from the generic "chablis" wines that serve to introduce so many of us to the pleasures of white table wines.

How it tastes: Sometimes a little sweet, but normally dry, fruity, refreshing, with a pleasing, perfumed aroma.

How to serve: An excellent luncheon wine for a chicken or shrimp salad; also, if it's not sweet, good with fish, chicken, turkey, veal, eggs prepared in many ways. Serve nicely chilled anytime, by itself.

Price: $2 to $4.

Who makes Chenin Blanc: Eighty or more California wineries; a few in Washington State. In California: Almadén, Beringer, Brookside, Burgess, Callaway, Chappellet, Christian Brothers, Concannon, Cresta Blanca, Dry Creek, Foppiano, Franciscan, Gallo, Geyser Peak, Korbel, Charles Krug, Louis M. Martini, Paul Masson, Mirassou, Robert Mondavi, San Martín, Simi, Sonoma, Souverain, Weibel, Wente. Also Ste. Michelle in Washington State.

Special note: Gallo's well-known Chablis Blanc white wine, available in "jug" sizes, contains roughly 60 percent Chenin Blanc grapes. It's a good, economical way to try this wine initially to see if you like it—although the Gallo is not quite so fruity as most varietal Chenin Blancs.

Chianti

(Key-ON-ti)

In Italy, this is a recognized fine red wine, but in America, the word may be applied to quite ordinary wines, sometimes sold in fancy bottles. On this side of the Atlantic, winemasters tend to make chianti somewhat sweeter than their burgundy—otherwise the distinction between the two is frequently slight. American wines containing the word "tipo" are chiantis, too.

How it tastes: Smooth and mellow in the better versions, ranging downward toward bland in the less expensive ones. Chianti typically contains less tannin and less acid than most other red wines, which explains its lack of pronounced flavor.

How to serve: With Italian dishes or hearty meals of any kind. You may prefer chianti at room temperature, rather than chilled; its flavors come out more distinctly then.

Price: $1.50 to $3. "Jug" sizes are available at a saving.

Who makes chianti: Almadén, Bargetto, Gallo, Italian Swiss Colony, San Martín, Sebastiani, Weibel, others.

Special note: Many wineries are now producing the better Italian-style varietals instead of generic chianti. See the listings under Barbera, Charbono, and Grignolino.

Cold Duck

A combination of sparkling red and white wines, usually quite sweet. Cold duck was a "fad" wine in the 1960s, but

its popularity has declined in recent years. Its name comes from a German pun based on the words kalte ende ("cold end," or "leftover") and kalte ente ("cold duck"). German partygoers poured together the leftover red and white wines and humorously called them cold duck. A Detroit restaurant began serving cold duck as a bar drink, and later it was bottled as an official (recognized by our Internal Revenue Service) wine category.

How it tastes. Bubbly to the extreme—even foamy—cold duck has little distinct flavor, other than its tendency toward sweetness. It is the "pop wine" of American champagnes.

How to serve: Beginning wine drinkers may be introduced to sparkling wines via cold duck, but they'll probably prefer either champagne or sparkling burgundy later on.

Price: Somewhat less than the above alternatives; $3 to $5.

Who makes cold duck: André, Christian Brothers, Eleven Cellars, Paul Masson, Taylor, others.

Special note: "Very Cold Duck" and "Extra Cold Duck" are just marketing ploys; the names have no special meaning.

Concord

The familiar blue "juice-and-jam" grape, a native American, it isn't a fine winemaking grape. Even so, its heavy, sweet, red wine is still enjoyed by many people. Eastern winemakers are now making Concord wines with less "grape jelly" character.

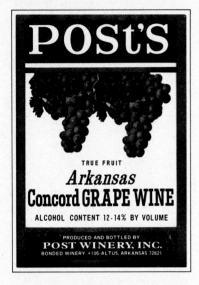

How it tastes: Usually sweet, very grapy of smell and taste—though some fairly dry Concord wines are blended with California wine or wine from hybrid grapes for a more pleasing aroma and flavor. White Concord wine is also made by removing the grape skins before fermentation.
How to serve: Most Concord wines are afternoon or evening wines, served without food. However, the dry red ones complement hamburgers, casseroles, or any everyday food.
Price: Usually under $2.50.
Who makes Concord: Michigan: Frontenac, St. Julian. New York: Canandaigua, Gold Seal, Royal Wine, Schapiro's, Widmer's. Illinois: Mogen David. Ohio: Meier's and numerous small wineries. Arkansas: Post's.

De Chaunac

(Duh-show-NOK)

A French hybrid used for red and rosé wines and named for the Canadian researcher most responsible for this grape's popularity in Ontario. The success of his vines sparked plantings in the Northeastern United States. A dozen or more American wineries now make a varietal De Chaunac wine. Others will follow when their vines mature and begin producing. The wine tends to be light in color unless blended; it is improved by aging in oak casks and in the bottle.

How it tastes: Dry red or pink wine of agreeable flavor; a little harsh when young. The better De Chaunac wines are aged and mellower.
How to serve: Good with roasts, meat loaf, stews, chops, and casseroles.
Price: Around $3.
Who makes De Chaunac: Indiana: Easley's, Villa Medo. Kentucky: Colcord. Michigan: Boskydel, Bronte, Fenn Valley, Warner. New Jersey: Tomasello. New York: Benmarl, Great Western, Merrit Estate, Royal Wine. Ohio: Valley Vineyards. Pennsylvania: Conoy.

Delaware

Valued for its resistance to cold weather as well as the quality of its wine, our native Delaware grape is also a good eating variety. The pinkish-red fruit yields white juice used in blends for Eastern sparkling wines, as well as for table wine. About 20 wineries make a varietal wine from Delaware grapes. The name comes from Delaware, Ohio, where the vine thrived, not from the state of Delaware.

How it tastes: Light golden in color, the wine is dry or semi-sweet and pleasantly soft and fruity.
How to serve: With luncheon foods or by itself, afternoon or evening.
Price: About $2.50.
Who makes Delaware: Arkansas: Center Ridge, Heckmann's, Post's. Michigan: Bronte, Frontenac. Missouri: Mt. Pleasant. New Jersey: Gross' Highland. New York: Barry, Johnson, Royal, Villa D'Ingianni, Widmer's. Ohio: Catawba Island, Cedar Hill, Chalet Debonne, Steuk. Pennsylvania: Doerflinger, Penn Shore, Presque Isle.

Dutchess

An American native grape that will probably be replaced by some hybrid in the future—not because it doesn't make good wine, but because the Dutchess vine lacks vigor and is subject to fungus diseases. Eastern growers receive high prices for delivering these grapes to a winery; the yellow-green fruit, delicious to eat, makes a clean, fruity wine without a trace of the unwanted "grape jelly" aroma and flavor that afflict so many of our native grapes.

How it tastes: An agreeable, fruity wine with a pleasing aroma and lingering aftertaste; usually moderately sweet.
How to serve: Good with fish and seafoods, chicken, veal, and ham.
Price: Around $2.
Who makes Dutchess: Indiana: Easley's. Michigan: Frontenac. New Jersey: Gross' Highland. New York: Great Western. Ohio: Cedar Hill. Pennsylvania: Bucks Country, Conestoga, Doerflinger, Mazza, Penn Shore, Presque Isle.

Emerald Riesling

(REEZ-ling)

A grape variety developed at the University of California at Davis, Emerald Riesling is well adapted to the hot Central Valley in that state. It's both productive and high in acid—a desirable quality usually lacking in grapes from warm regions.

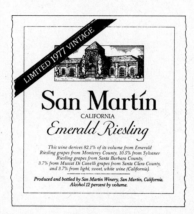

How it tastes: Crisp, clean, refreshing. A very good, inexpensive white wine.
How to serve: Drink it as an appetizer or serve with fish and seafood, fish or chicken salads, casseroles, cold cuts.
Price: $2 to $2.50.
Who makes Emerald Riesling: Bear Mountain, Bronco, Brookside, California Growers, East Side, Galleano, Giumarra, Monterey Vineyard, Rapazzini, San Antonio, San Martín.
Special note: Paul Masson makes a very nice Emerald Dry wine that is a blend of predominantly Emerald Riesling grapes. Despite its name, this wine has a touch of sweetness, in the German manner.

Foch (or Maréchal Foch)

(Mar-ay-shahl FOSH)

Blue-black hybrid grapes of Alsatian (French) origin and the superior garnet wine they make. The Gamay grape is related to Foch. The wine itself is subtle and complex, qualities that take some aging to develop.

How it tastes: When young, it is harsh and biting, with an excess of tannin. After aging in oak and bottle, a softer but hearty wine emerges, full bodied and somewhat spicy in flavor.
How to serve: With roasts and pot roasts, spaghetti, lasagna, cold cuts, many foods.
Price: About $2.50 to $3.50.
Who makes Maréchal Foch: Michigan: Bronte, Tabor Hill, Warner. Missouri: Green Valley. New Jersey: Gross' Highland. New York: Benmarl, Merrit, Widmer's. Ohio: Sublette, Valley Vineyards. Pennsylvania: Penn Shore. Virginia: Meredyth Vineyards.

French Colombard

A prolific white wine grape from California's Central Valley, French Colombard makes a delicious everyday wine. Modern technology has been responsible for the quality of this wine, which is far superior to what might be expected from such a hot climate. It's fermented at lower-than-normal temperatures in stainless steel tanks in order to preserve the light, delicate flavor. As a result, an increasing number of California wineries has begun to make French Colombard now that its popularity is apparent.

How it tastes: The pale, green-gold wine has just enough acid to stimulate the taste buds immediately. It is *juicy* wine, fresh and light, enjoyable.

How to serve: As an appetizer, or with light foods such as tuna or chicken salad, cold cuts and cheese, salmon or chicken loaf, picnic fare.

Price: $2 to $3.50.

Who makes French Colombard: About 35 California wineries, including: Almadén, Brookside, California Growers, Cresta Blanca, Foppiano, Franzia, Gallo, Inglenook, M. La Mont, Paul Masson, Parducci, Sonoma, Souverain, Winemaster's Guild.

Special note: Consider having a party featuring French Colombard. It may be a simple little wine, but not everyone is familiar with it and nearly everybody *likes* it!

Fruit Wines

Wine, in its simplest definition, is the fermented juice of the grape. Other fruits do not turn themselves into wine quite so naturally. They usually need the help of sugar to overcome their acids, and sometimes they require dilution with water. Most fruit wines do not keep very well, either, so they should be consumed within a year.

The cherry wines of Wisconsin can be delicious when not too sweet, and several wineries in Michigan and California have earned reputations for wines made of native fruits such as strawberries, peaches, and apples. Iowa's Amana colonies produce piestengl (rhubarb) and several other fruit wines that may be sold only on the premises as "homemade." Are these really wines? It's a moot point. Many people enjoy them, so it hardly matters.

Fruit wines are seldom served with meals. The sweetest of them usually function as cordials. Some are delicious on mixtures of fresh fruit, served as dessert.

Fumé Blanc (Blanc Fumé) (Napa Fumé)

(Foo-may BLAWN)

All of these names are alternates of Sauvignon Blanc (see that listing on page 39 for complete details).

The French word "fumé" means "smoked." In this country, Fumé Blanc wine is not smoked nor does it have a smoky taste or appearance. It is simply a delightful, very dry white wine.

In the French Loire Valley, however, the ripe Sauvignon Blanc grapes take on a smoky hue, and some say you can even taste a subtle smokiness in the wine. American winemasters, beginning with Robert Mondavi, liked the sound of the Fumé name and found that many American buyers did, too. But it does create some problems of identification when essentially the same wine is produced under so many different names.

Gamay (Napa Gamay) (Gamay Noir)

(Gam-MAY NWAR)

Although there has been some confusion in California among these, it is now understood that the red wine grapes known as Gamay, Napa Gamay, or Gamay Noir are descendants of the true Gamay grapes of the French Beaujolais district. Gamay Beaujolais, despite its name, is related to the Pinot Noir grape of French Burgundy. Gamay needs no aging and is best consumed fresh. Rosé wines, too, are sometimes made of Gamay grapes.

How it tastes: Gamay is light and fruity, fresh and pleasant. It's often called a "happy wine."
How to serve: With a ham sandwich, fried chicken, a meat and vegetable casserole, pork or lamb chops, ribs, cold cuts.
Price: $2.50 to $4.
Who makes Gamay: More than 30 California wineries, including: Alamadén, Beringer, California Growers, Christian Brothers, Franciscan, Geyser Peak, Paul Masson, Mondavi, Trentadue. Presque Isle in Pennsylvania.

Gamay Beaujolais

(Gam-MAY BO-zho-lay)

As explained on page 25, the *Gamay Beaujolis grape is not the grape of Beaujolais but is actually a Pinot Noir (see that listing, too). Yet in this country, the wine is often made like a young French Beaujolais—very fresh and fruity, for immediate consumption. Some wineries label their wine "nouveau" or "primeur"; such bottles should be consumed within six months of fermentation. Most other Gamay Beaujolais may be expected to keep well for two or three years, though it is not a particularly good wine to lay away in a cellar for aging.*

How it tastes: "Nouveau" tastes very fresh, high in acid, and has a fruity aroma. It is a quaffing wine, not one to carefully sip and savor. A vintage Gamay Beaujolais, on the other hand, is a less fruity, softer red wine that's very pleasing in a different way.

How to serve: "Nouveau" is a festive picnic wine. Serve it with cheese or snack food, or a light lunch or supper. Other Gamay Beaujolais goes well with ham, steaks, chops, stew, and combinations such as meat balls served on rice or noodles.

Price: $3 to $4.

Who makes Gamay Beaujolais: More than 40 California wineries, including: Almadén, Beaulieu, Beringer, Cresta Blanca, Fetzer, Inglenook, Krug, Louis M. Martini, Paul Masson, Mirassou, Monterey Vineyard, Parducci, San Martín, Sebastiani, Simi, Sonoma, Souverain, Weibel, Wente. Also Washington: Ste. Michelle.

Gewürztraminer

(Geh-vertz-tra-MEAN-er or Geh-woors-tra-mean-AIR, as the French pronounce it)

A tough-skinned, pinkish-blue grape of the French Alsace region and the American West Coast; it makes a distinctive, perfumed, spicy white wine. Gewürztraminer vines are not highly productive, and this wine isn't easy to make. Still, excellent examples are appearing in California, Washington, and Oregon, some of them a little sweet. (Gewürztraminer is usually produced as a fairly dry wine in France.) As a result, this wine is growing very rapidly in popularity; it appears to have a bright future on this side of the Atlantic.

Inglenook

NAPA VALLEY
GEWÜRZTRAMINER

A soft delicate white table wine with the spicy aroma and brisk taste of the Gewürztraminer grape variety.

Produced and Bottled by Inglenook Vineyards Rutherford, California. Alcohol 12% by Vol.

How it tastes: Decidedly spicy and aromatic—there's no mistaking this wine. It's the one you'll remember as "perfumy," and for some people it takes a while to appreciate.

How to serve: With spicy or well-seasoned foods, such as Alsatian sauerkraut with smoked meats and sausage (*choucroute garnie*), a light curry, roast pork, ham, barbecued ribs or chicken, cold meat and cheese tray.

Price: $3 to $4.

Who makes Gewürztraminer: These and other California wineries: Almadén, Buena Vista, Christian Brothers, Cresta Blanca, Firestone, Krug, Louis M. Martini, Paul Masson, Mirassou, Monterey Vineyard, Pedroncelli, Phelps, Sebastiani, Simi, Souverain. Michigan: Fenn Valley. Oregon: Tualatin. Washington: Associated Vintners, Ste. Michelle, others.

Special note: If your food seasoning is *too hot,* a Gewürztraminer (and most other wines) can be overwhelmed; don't waste such a lovely wine on a really hot curry, chili, or similar fiery dishes.

Green Hungarian

A white wine grape of uncertain origin, except that it certainly doesn't come from Hungary; it makes a fairly bland but pleasant wine in California. Green Hungarian is commonly used in blends for California chablis, and about 20 wineries make a varietal wine of it as well. Usually this wine is dry, but a few wineries, such as the Weibel shown here, leave some residual sugar for a sweet taste. Several wineries even make a sparkling wine from it.

VINEYARDS ESTABLISHED 1825
1977
Sebastiani
FOUNDED AT THE END OF EL CAMINO REAL

NORTHERN CALIFORNIA
GREEN HUNGARIAN
Semi-Dry and Fragrant

VINTED AND BOTTLED BY SEBASTIANI VINEYARDS
SONOMA VALLEY, CALIFORNIA 95476
ALC. 12% BY VOL. BONDED WINERY 876

How it tastes: Pleasingly fruity and fragrant, it's the kind of white wine most people like.

How to serve: As an appetizer wine, or with chicken or meat salad, egg dishes, most luncheon food. It also complements the taste of fresh fruit very well.

Price: $2.50 to $4.

Who makes Green Hungarian: Buena Vista, Burgess, California Growers, M. La Mont, Parducci, Pedrizetti, Sebastiani, Souverain, Weibel, Winemaster's Guild, and others.

Grenache

(Gren-AHSH)

Dark, reddish-purple grapes of the kind that thrive in France's Provence region and also in Spain, where they are called Garnacha. The wine they make is light red, so it's used in California as a blending wine and for rosé wines. The vine is prolific in the hot Central Valley of California, so there should be no shortage of this attractive wine with a trace of orange under its rosiness.

How it tastes: It can be deliciously fruity and fresh—much better when the winery makes it dry rather than sweet.
How to serve: With a jellied shrimp salad, a platter of deviled eggs, all of summer's informal foods. A good picnic wine.
Price: $2 to $3.
Who makes Grenache rosé: More than 40 California wineries, including: Almadén, Beaulieu, Brookside, Burgess, Cresta Blanca, Franzia, Inglenook, M. La Mont, Paul Masson, San Martín, Sebastiani, Sonoma, Souverain, Weibel. Washington: Ste. Michelle.

Grey Riesling

(REEZ-ling)

A fair white wine grape (actually not a true Riesling) that makes a soft wine without much distinction. It was more popular a few years ago than it is now; but Grey Riesling still has its partisans, and about 20 California wineries make it.

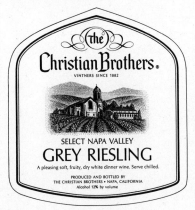

How it tastes: Agreeable, usually pleasantly dry.
How to serve: With any dishes that aren't too elegant. Grey Riesling does have the ability to go with a wide variety of foods and flavors.
Price: $2.50 to $3.50.
Who makes Grey Riesling: Almadén, Beringer, Buena Vista, California Growers, Christian Brothers, Cresta Blanca, Korbel, Krug, Sonoma, Souverain, Weibel, Wente, and others.

Grignolino

(Green-yo-LEAN-o)

A wine grape of Italy's Piedmont district that makes a light-bodied, light red wine with piquant flavor and perfumed aroma. Some California wineries make it as a rosé wine. Grignolino's color is quite unusual, both as a red wine and a rosé—it is tinged with orange.

How it tastes: Distinctively different, with its aroma of flowers and fruit; dry, tart, pungent.
How to serve: With a roast of lamb or pork, duck, pheasant. Grignolino's combination of tartness and astringency also makes it a good choice with pasta and other well-seasoned tomato dishes. The rosé goes well with shrimp, lobster, other seafood.
Price: $3 to $5.
Who makes Grignolino: Beringer, Bertero, Guglielmo, Heitz, Thomas Kruse. In addition to its regular Grignolino, Beringer makes a blend of Grignolino and Pinot Noir, which this winery has named Berenblut.
Special note: Grignolino is still somewhat of a connoisseur's wine. It isn't well known yet, though most of its winemakers give it special care.

Johannisberg Riesling

(Yo-hon-iss-berg REEZ-ling)

Here is a case where one American wine has two names—Johannisberg Riesling and White Riesling—and they are about equally common. Because the name White Riesling avoids any possible confusion with the famous old German Schloss Johannisberg wine, the American version is listed in detail under "Riesling, White" on page 36.

There are several other "Riesling" wines made in this

country. Emerald Riesling (page 23) is a special California hybrid developed in this century. Grey Riesling (page 29) is not in the Riesling family at all but comes from an unrelated French grape. If you find a U.S. wine labeled simply "Riesling," with no further designation, it probably was made from Sylvaner (also known as Franken Riesling) grapes (page 42)—and they are only distantly related to the White or Johannisberg Riesling.

Although most American "Rieslings" are very drinkable white wines, the superior quality of White Riesling is immediately evident in comparison. The price reflects the quality.

Malvasia Bianca

(Mal-va-zee-a Bee-AHN-ka)

An ancient and distinguished member of the large family of Muscat grapes, this is the one used to make the famous fortified wine of the island of Madeira, known as "Malmsey." In California, however, it makes an entirely different wine that is growing in popularity. Here, the typical Malvasia Bianca is a light, sweet white wine of 12½ percent alcohol or less.

How it tastes: Rich and rather heavy, with the distinctive "ripe fruit" fragrance that's characteristic of Muscat grapes.
How to serve: Well chilled, by itself in the afternoon or evening, or with a dessert such as apple, pear, peach or berry tarts, or fruit cake or pound cake.
Price: $2 to $3.
Who makes Malvasia Bianca: Beringer, Brookside, Kirigin, Novitiate, San Martín, Monterey Vineyard, Pastori, Stony Ridge, Villa Armando.

Merlot

(Mare-LO)

A very fine red wine grape once grown primarily for blending with Cabernet Sauvignon. Today in California, it is increasingly being used to make a varietal red wine.

Its role in blending has been to soften and round out Cabernet Sauvignon, which tends to mature slowly by itself. Merlot has much of the same richness and fine character of Cabernet, but they develop quite a bit faster. Even so, Merlot benefits from careful handling by the winemaster, who should not rush it to the consumer before it's ready. As a result, Merlot is more costly to produce than most other popular California red wines.

Many producers age Merlot in oak, then follow with another period of bottle aging before releasing the wine for sale—at which time it is ready to drink. You probably won't add much to its already fine character if you age a bottle of Merlot yourself.

How it tastes: A rich, ruby wine that may have an herb-like overtone in its fruity flavor. Some think it has a bit of the aroma and taste of black currants as well.
How to serve: With lamb, beef,

duck, game birds, and cheese such as Brie and Camembert. Merlot, like Cabernet Sauvignon, is an elegant wine suitable for an elegant occasion.
Price: $4 to $9.

Who makes Merlot: Burgess, Davis Bynum, Chappellet, Chateau St. Jean, Dry Creek, Firestone, Gundlach-Bundschu, Louis M. Martini, Papagni, Joseph Phelps, Souverain, Stag's Leap, Sterling, Stonegate, Trentadue, York Mountain, other California wineries. New York: Long Island Vineyards. Oregon: Charles Coury, Eyrie. Pennsylvania: Presque Isle. Washington: Ste. Michelle, others.

Special note: Most producers of Merlot are small wineries aiming for high quality. The wine appears to have a bright future, and prices will probably come down as more Merlot is produced.

Muscat (Moscato) (Muscatel)

The Muscat family is a very large one that produces a wide variety of white or amber wines—most of them sweet, a few on the dry side.

In the past, it was common to fortify all Muscat wines with brandy to bring the alcohol content to around 17 or 18 percent, as in the case of muscatel. The new trend in California is to make lighter, unfortified wines of about 11 or 12 percent alcohol from Muscat grapes. These wines go by names such as Muscat

Blanc, Moscato di Canelli (Mus-KAHT-o de Ka-NELL-ee), or Muscat Frontignan (Mus-ket FRAWN-teen-yan).

These recent developments spring from today's strong demand for white table wines—coupled with the great productivity of the Muscat vines. Many wine drinkers find the unfortified Muscats to be a pleasant change from the usually undistinguished chablis or rhine so often served in place of cocktails.

For taste and serving information, turn the page.

How it tastes: Be careful to check the alcohol content on the label, because there's wide variation between the fortified (17 to 18 percent) and unfortified (11 to 12 percent) versions of these wines.

All Muscat wines are flowery and fragrant, with an aroma often described as that of "ripe fruit." Beyond that, a low alcohol content may indicate a dry wine or one that's semi-sweet—check the front or back label on these points, too. Fortified Muscat wines are *always* sweet; muscatel usually reminds you of sweet raisins.

How to serve: Dry Muscat wines may be used as appetizers, much the same as other white table wines. Semi-sweet Muscats go well with pastry or fruit at the table. Serve both of these lower-alcohol wines well chilled.

Sweet, fortified Muscats such as muscatel are dessert wines that should be served in small glasses at room temperature.

Price: $3 to $6.50 for the unfortified Muscats with the variety of names listed earlier. $1.50 to $3 for most sweet muscatels.

Who makes Muscat (Blanc, Canelli, Frontignan, and others): Beaulieu, Chateau St. Jean, Christian Brothers (Chateau LaSalle), Concannon, Cresta Blanca, Franciscan, Charles Krug, Robert Mondavi, Angelo Papagni, San Martin, Simi, Souverain, Sutter Home, others. Sweet muscatel is made by Gallo and other high-volume producers—frequently in jug size.

Special note: In Italy, this same grape is used to make the famous Asti Spumante sparkling wine.

Niagara

Native Eastern, light green grape; it makes a pale yellow wine that ranges from very ordinary to quite good. New varieties, mostly hybrids, are now available to replace Niagara, but this wine is still made by more than 20 Eastern wineries—most successfully by Widmer's (Lake Niagara) and Great Western.

PREMIUM NEW YORK STATE
WHITE NIAGARA
Golden mellow, fruity
light table wine.

PRODUCED AND BOTTLED BY PLEASANT VALLEY WINE COMPANY
ALCOHOL 12% BY VOLUME   HAMMONDSPORT, N.Y. 14840

How it tastes: Quite fruity, somewhat "grape juicy." Some Niagaras have a soda-pop flavor that younger wine drinkers like.
How to serve: Well chilled, Niagara is refreshing as an afternoon cooler on hot days. It's better served by itself than with meals.
Price: $2 to $3.
Who makes Niagara: New York: Barry Wine Co., Canandaigua, Great Western, Merritt Estate, Royal Wine Corp., Widmer's. Ohio: Catawba Island, Chalet Debonne, Valley Vineyards. Michigan: Bronte, St. Julian.

Petite Sirah
(Puh-TEET Sear-RAH)

A heavily pigmented, red wine grape widely grown in California. Once thought to be the Syrah grape of the Rhone Valley in France, it's now believed to be another grape, the Duriff. (A small number of California wineries apparently do grow the true Syrah grape.)

Formerly used only to give more color and body to other wines, Petite Sirah is now being made on its own as a full-bodied, deep-colored varietal wine that ages well. Its popularity is still growing, and as more Petite Sirah is produced year by year, its price has also become more reasonable.

Sonoma Vineyards
1975 Petite Sirah
Northern California
PRODUCED AND BOTTLED AT THE WINERY BY SONOMA VINEYARDS
WINDSOR, SONOMA COUNTY, CALIFORNIA. ALCOHOL 12% BY VOLUME

How it tastes: The less expensive Petite Sirahs are somewhat light and fruity; going up in price tends to give you more body and color. The heavier wines are very tannic (astringent) when young, but as they age, they smooth out. A pungent, peppery flavor is characteristic of the best ones, which are also very aromatic.

How to serve: Good with beef and lamb stews, barbecued meats, well-seasoned dishes of many kinds. Petite Sirah is a bold, vigorous wine that can stand up to (and complement) foods with strong or distinctive flavors of their own.

Price: $2.50 to $7. Excellent quality at around $5.

Who makes Petite Sirah: Nearly 60 wineries, mostly in California, including: Almadén, Brookside, Burgess, Callaway, Chateau St. Jean, Concannon (first to make it), Cresta Blanca, Dry Creek, Fetzer, Poppiano, Paul Masson, Mirassou, Phelps (true Syrah grape), Sonoma, Weibel, Wente.

Pinot Blanc
(Pea-no BLAWN)

A white wine grape of excellent quality, which makes a fine wine somewhat resembling Chardonnay. Like Chardonnay, it develops best when grown in the cool coastal vineyards of California. Some vintners age Pinot Blanc for a few months in oak before bottling it.

How it tastes: Dry, similar to Chardonnay, with a faint hint of apple, pear, or melon.

How to serve: With lobster, crab, shrimp, oysters on the half shell, chicken or turkey, veal.

Price: $4 to $5.

Who makes Pinot Blanc: Almadén, Chalone, Chateau St. Jean, Paul Masson, Mirassou, Novitiate, Sebastiani, Turgeon and Lohr, Wente, others.

Special note: Pinot Blanc is gradually being phased out in California in favor of Chardonnay, which has become much more popular as a premium quality white wine in recent years.

Pinot Noir

(Pea-no NWAR)

One of the two grape aristocrats (the other is Cabernet Sauvignon) from which the world's best red wines are made. It is also the grape of the Burgundy and Champagne districts of France.

There have been difficulties in growing Pinot Noir vines and making the wine in California, and you'll still find quite a variation in quality from one winery to another. Nearly 100 wineries are now making varietal Pinot Noir; many of the wines are very fine. A few wineries make Rosé of Pinot Noir; several even make white wine from these grapes.

How it tastes: When given several years to age in cask and bottle, a good Pinot Noir is silky and complex in character, with a perfumed aroma and a taste that somewhat resembles ripe plums.

How to serve: With roast beef, venison, duck, wild duck, and goose—if the wine is a big, full, aged one. A light-bodied, fruity, young Pinot Noir is better with informal foods, even including hamburger.

Price: $3.50 to $6.

Who makes Pinot Noir: Almadén, Beaulieu, Beringer, Buena Vista, Cresta Blanca, Geyser Peak, Krug, Louis M. Martini, Paul Masson, Mirassou,

1975

Charles Krug

NAPA VALLEY
PINOT NOIR

PRODUCED AND BOTTLED BY
Charles Krug Winery
ST. HELENA · CALIFORNIA
ALCOHOL 12% BY VOLUME

Robert Mondavi, Monterey Vineyard, Sebastiani, Simi, Sonoma, Souverain, Wente, many other California wineries. Indiana: Banholzer. Oregon: Tualatin, others. Washington: Associated Vintners, others.

Special note: The best years of Pinot Noir wine in California are probably yet to come. More and more of these temperamental vines are being planted in cool hillside areas where they seem to produce more reliably. New experiments on early harvesting and aging (both with and without oak casks) hint at a still varied but more robust and flavorful future for Pinot Noir.

"Pop" Wines

Highly favored by American youth a few years ago, these "pop" (as in "soda pop") wines have steadily lost ground. However, Annie Green Springs (United Vintners) and Boone's Farm

(Gallo) wines, with names like Strawberry Hill, Apricot Splash, and Tickle Pink, are still around, performing their role of transitional beverage between teen soft drinks and table wines.

"Pop" wines usually have a grape or apple wine base that's somewhat sweet, light in alcohol (8 to 11 percent), and often lightly carbonated. Any added flavor must be natural and may be cherry, berry, peach, or another fruit with an appealing taste.

Port

"Port" in the United States bears little resemblance to the famous sweet red Port wine of Portugal—other than being a sweet red wine itself, fortified with brandy to raise the alcohol to 18 to 21 percent.

California ports are easily the best in this country, especially the few made with Portuguese varieties of grapes, such as tinta madeira, tinta cao, or souzao. These varieties thrive in the hot valleys, as do two grapes, rubired and royalty, developed by the University of California at Davis, especially for ports.

How it tastes: California port is made in three basic styles: *ruby,* a deep red, fruity wine; *tawny,* an amber-colored wine; and *white* port, which has a fruity aroma and golden color.
How to serve: Serve port in the afternoon or evening, with nuts or light desserts or fruit cake. For hot mulled wine, warm a bottle of port and a bottle of everyday red wine ("burgundy") with a few cloves, a cinnamon stick, and several slices of lemon or orange. Sweeten with sugar syrup to taste, and serve this wine recipe hot in mugs.
Price: $1.50 to $6.
Who makes port: Among the best are the Christian Brothers, Ficklin, Llords and Elwood, Paul Masson, and J. W. Morris.

Rhine

Like "chablis" and "sauterne," the name "rhine" has little specific meaning when applied to American white wines. But the word persists here, even though rhine is gradually giving way to more descriptive varietal wines, like French Colombard and Chenin Blanc. Each of these has a fresh, juicy flavor, which "rhine" promises but doesn't always deliver in this country.

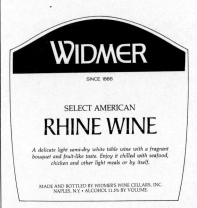

How it tastes: A rhine from Vineyard X tends to be somewhat sweeter than the chablis from Vineyard X; sample several brands to get a wine you like. Most American rhines are pleasant but not very exciting.
How to serve: With luncheon salads, poultry dishes, light or non-spicy recipes.
Price: $1.50 to $3.
Who makes rhine: The large California bottlers such as Almadén, Christian Brothers, Eleven Cellars, Gallo, Paul Masson. New York: Gold Seal, Taylor. Arkansas: Post's.
Special note: A jug of chilled rhine wine makes a good base for a white wine punch. Mix it with two or three parts cold sparkling water and perhaps a little creme de cassis, and garnish with fresh orange slices.

Riesling, White or Johannisberg

(Yo-HAN-nis-berg REEZ-ling)

Both names refer to the noble grape of Germany's Rhine and Mosel Rivers, now cultivated in every wine-growing country cool enough to be favorable for it. (See also page 30.)

Riesling grapes make what is considered one of the two best white wines in the world—Chardonnay is the other. As they ripen, the small green grapes may be afflicted with "noble rot." This beneficial mold, botrytis cinerea, shrivels the grapes and concentrates their juices, so the wine made from them is rich and luscious.

TABOR HILL

Johannisberg Riesling

Produced and bottled by
Tabor Hill Vineyard and Winecellars, Inc.
Buchanan, Berrien County, Michigan 49107
Alcohol 11% by volume.

How it tastes: Young, fresh White Riesling has a floral aroma, a clean fruity taste, and a good balance of acidity along with its slight sweetness. Late Harvest White Riesling is richer, heavier of body, and has a honeyed fragrance.

How to serve: With fish and seafood, veal, chicken, turkey, cold cuts, and sausages (as in Germany and Alsace). Late Harvest White Riesling is best served without food.

Price: $3.50 to $5.50—more for Late Harvest bottles.

Who makes White (Johannisberg) Riesling: Almost all California wineries of the North Coast. Washington and Oregon wineries, including: Ste. Michelle, Tualatin. Michigan: Fenn Valley, Tabor Hill. Ohio: Markko. Others in New York, Pennsylvania, Wisconsin.

Rosé Wines

(Ro-ZAY)

Rosé wines are simply pale red wines; the grape skins are removed early in fermentation, before all the usual red color can develop in the wine. Rosé may be sweet or dry, or even lightly carbonated. Some rosés are blends of many grapes and are usually called simply "vin rosé"; others are specific varietals.

A number of California wineries are making exceptional rosé wines from fine red wine grapes such as Cabernet Sauvignon, Pinot Noir, Grignolino, Gamay,

and Zinfandel. The earliest California pink wines were made of Grenache grapes, and several excellent ones still are (see page 29).

A few California vintners are trying a new method—really a white wine process applied to the deep red Pinot Noir grapes. Color comes from the crushed grapes only; the skins and seeds are removed before fermentation (see "How Wine Is Made," page 52). For taste and serving information on rosé wines, turn the page.

How it tastes: There are as many tastes as there are grapes and blends of rosé. The finest of them are dry, fruity, fresh tasting. Rosé wines are at their most flavorful, with loveliest color, within two years of vintage—so don't try to age them.

How to serve: Well chilled, with ham, fried chicken, picnic foods. The more sophisticated varietals, with lobster and other shellfish; cold, rare beef; lamb chops; duck.

Price: About $2.50 or less for most; the special varietals range up to $4.

Who makes rosé wine: Almost all wineries; some make two or three kinds. Shop around!

Special note: It isn't a sin to add ice cubes, lemon twist, and sparkling water to a sweet rosé wine on a hot summer day. But a really fine one, such as Rosé of Cabernet Sauvignon, should be savored as carefully as any other classic wine.

Ruby Cabernet
(Ruby Kab-er-NAY)

A cross of Cabernet and Carignane developed at the University of California-Davis for better adaptability to climate. Now grown extensively in the Central Valley of California, Ruby Cabernet makes very good "ordinary" red wines that are in abundant supply. You can often buy Ruby Cabernet in big bottles at a savings.

How it tastes: Dry, fruity, and refreshing. It's an everyday wine, not an elegant wine; very pleasant.

How to serve: With picnic fare, simple meals of all kinds, including sandwiches (even hot dogs and hamburgers).

Price: Around $2 or even less.

Who makes Ruby Cabernet: Almadén, Brookside, California Growers, Cresta Blanca, Franzia, Gallo, Italian Swiss Colony, M. La Mont, Paul Masson, Sonoma, United Vintners, Winemaster's Guild, other California wineries.

Special note: Ruby Cabernet provides a satisfying alternative to burgundy for confirmed red wine drinkers. Its price is not much higher, and its flavor is more distinct and pleasing than the burgundy blends widely available on the market.

Sangria
(San-GREE-a)

Most Americans first heard of Sangria as a result of the popular Spanish Pavilion at the New York World's Fair in the early 1960s. Essentially a Spanish red wine "lemonade," Sangria has been bottled and marketed successfully by several American wineries. The flavor, superimposed on a red wine base, usually is a blend of citrus—supplied by

oranges and lemons.

It's also possible to make your own Sangria. Pour a bottle of red wine, burgundy for instance, into a big pitcher, add 2 tablespoons sugar, a few lemon and orange slices, some ice cubes, and sparkling water. Serve in wine glasses.

Sauterne

(Saw-TERN)

A generic term now falling into disuse in this country. It usually indicates a white wine with some sweetness, but otherwise it bears little resemblance to a great Sauternes (always with the final "s") of France. California vintners are phasing it out; in the East, sauterne often is made from native American grapes, with quite variable results.

How it tastes: Varies widely—sometimes sweet but usually dry. Eastern sauternes are often made with strong-flavored native American grapes.

How to serve: It's appropriate with baked chicken or turkey, ham, tuna, or salmon dishes.

Price: $2 to $4. Also available in larger bottles at a savings.

WIDMER

SINCE 1888

SELECT AMERICAN
SAUTERNE

A crisp semi-dry white table wine that is both delicate in flavor and beautiful to the eye. Enjoy it chilled as an aperitif or as an honorable accompaniment to light foods, particularly fish and seafood.

MADE AND BOTTLED BY WIDMER'S WINE CELLARS, INC.
NAPLES, N.Y. • ALCOHOL 11.5% BY VOLUME.

Who makes sauterne: Mostly the big-volume producers. In California: Almadén, Christian Brothers, Eleven Cellars, Gallo—plus Concannon, Louis M. Martini, and Wente. New York: Taylor, Widmer.

Sauvignon Blanc

(SO-vee-nyawn BLAWN)

Also known as Fumé Blanc and Blanc Fumé (see page 25), which are other French names for the same grape. This excellent white wine of classical quality is rapidly growing in popularity. The vines favor the coolest parts of California, and they do well in Washington and Oregon. About 50 wineries now make this wine under its various names; production is expected to increase. For taste and serving information, turn the page.

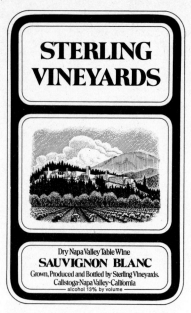

How it tastes: Dry, aromatic, a little spicy, very fruity. It takes some people a while to appreciate the quality of this wine, but, like a good friend, it usually grows on you with time.

How to serve: With fine fish as well as seafood, veal, turkey, chicken, ham.

Price: From under $2 to $7 or more.

Who makes Sauvignon Blanc and Fumé Blanc: At the lowest prices, Gallo makes an excellent Sauvignon Blanc. Other big producers, at medium prices, include Almadén, Christian Brothers (Napa Fumé), Inglenook. More expensive bottles come from (* indicates Fumé in the name on the label) Callaway, Dry Creek*, Mondavi*, Sterling, Spring Mountain, Joseph Phelps.*

Special note: A few wineries make this wine under more than one name, in different styles. The Fumé is usually drier, with a crisper flavor, than the Sauvignon Blanc. You may enjoy trying several versions before you pick a favorite.

Scuppernong

A grape of the Muscadine family, which grows in clusters like cherries instead of in bunches, and wine made from it. This native American vine grows wild in the Carolinas, as well as parts of Virginia, Florida, and Georgia.

How it tastes: This wine is pungently different, with a strong, somewhat bitter flavor. Most Scuppernong looks and tastes like sherry, being light amber in color and sherry-like in aroma.

How to serve: Usually it is made as a dessert wine, but recently some experiments have shown that Scuppernong has possibilities as a table wine. Country ham baked in Scuppernong wine is a rare treat.

Price: Around $2.

Who makes Scuppernong: You won't find it readily—Richard's Wine Cellars in South Carolina, Mother Vineyard in Virginia, Post's in Arkansas, and several small wineries in North Carolina make it.

Scuppernong is particularly interesting because it has been made almost continuously in its native territory since the earliest colonial times.

Semillon

(SAY-me-yawn)

This excellent white grape is blended with Sauvignon Blanc to make the great French Sauternes—those lusciously sweet wines of normal table-wine alcohol content. Not widely planted in California, Semillon is made by about a dozen wineries in that state, plus a few in Washington and Oregon. It may be fermented dry or sweet; check the label.

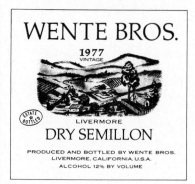

How it tastes: Fruity, sometimes tasting faintly of herbs. Sweeter Semillons often have an aroma reminiscent of ripe figs.

How to serve: Dry Semillon goes with fish and luncheon foods; sweet versions with fruit (or fruit and cheese for dessert).

Price: Around $3.

Who makes Semillon: Almadén, California Growers, Concannon, Novitiate, Wente, and a few other California wineries. Washington: Associated Vintners, Ste. Michelle. Oregon: Tualatin.

Special note: Semillon is occasionally blended with Sauvignon Blanc in this country and given a proprietary name, such as Chateau Such-and-Such. This is usually a sweet dessert wine. A few wineries still call such a wine "Haut Sauterne."

Seyval Blanc

(SAY-voll BLAWN)

French-American hybrid grapes that make an excellent white wine. (Chardonnay is in its parentage.) This wine is good when young and fresh. It also ages well in casks, developing additional flavor from the wood.

Most authorities see a great future for Seyval Blanc. So far, about 40 Midwestern and Eastern wineries produce it; others have vineyard plantings that are not yet fully developed. It appears to have that rare combination of hardiness to the climate extremes of our East and Midwest, along with fine flavor that's free of "grape jelly" overtones, which wines from our native vines often retain.

How it tastes: Crisp, fresh, and fruity—with a pleasing aroma of apples, like that characteristic of some Chardonnays.

How to serve: With fresh fish and seafood, chicken, turkey, veal, ham. It is a versatile wine.

Price: About $3.50.

Who makes Seyval Blanc: Indiana: Banholzer, Easley's, Villa Medeo. Michigan: Boskydel, Bronte, Fenn Valley, Leelanau, St. Julian, Tabor Hill, Warner. New York: Benmarl, Bully Hill, Johnson Estate. Ohio: Catawba Island, Mantey, Sublette, Valley Vineyards. Pennsylvania: Adams County, Bucks Country, Doerflinger, Penn Shore, Pequea Valley, Presque Isle. Virginia: Farfelu, Meredyth Vineyard. Wisconsin: Wollersheim.

Sherry

Sherries are helping to replace cocktails for many Americans, and our American wineries are producing some excellent ones. There are two basic types: dry sherry, an appetizer for before meals, and cream sherry, a dessert wine. A few producers here imitate the original Spanish method of blending sherries over the years in a solera—which is a system of stacking casks of wine in tiers, with the oldest wine at the bottom and the youngest at the top. As wine is drawn from the lowest casks, wine is added to them from the next-lowest tier, and that level in turn draws from the casks above. This process goes on "forever," and is one of the secrets of fine sherry flavor.

Sherry is a fortified wine, which means that grape brandy is added before bottling to bring the alcohol content to 17 to 21 percent by volume.

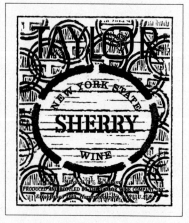

How it tastes: Dry sherry has a rich, heavy flavor, often nutty or woody from its casks. Cream sherry is sweeter but not overwhelmingly so in quality bottlings. Both fill the mouth with wine aromas and bouquets—a little sherry goes a long way!

How to serve: Dry sherry goes with appetizers—even garlicky, oniony, very spicy kinds—and all types of pickles. It should be served cold (some people even like it on the rocks). Cream sherry may be served either cold or at room temperature. If you'd like to reduce the sweetness a bit, add a twist of lemon or orange, plus some of the juice.
Price: $2 to $4.
Who makes sherry: California: Almadén, Concannon, Beaulieu (these three use the *solera* method for some of their sherries; check the labels), Gallo, Christian Brothers, Paul Masson, others. New York: Gold Seal, Great Western, Taylor, Widmer's. Ohio: Meier's.
Special note: Some wineries call their dry version "cocktail sherry." You may also find a medium-sweet "golden sherry." And if the label says only "sherry," with no qualifying word, it's probably medium-sweet.

Sylvaner
(Sil-VAHN-er)

The Sylvaner grape makes a pleasant white wine, but it's not quite up to the quality of White Riesling. In this country, it has not yet reached the level of its German heritage. But a pleasant white wine is not to be denigrated in this age of worship of white wines—there can't be too many!

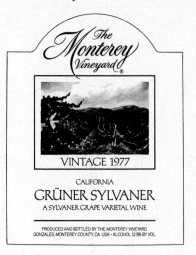

How it tastes: Fresh, dry, crisp, a little fruity.
How to serve: With all kinds of fish, chicken, turkey, ham, veal, luncheon dishes.
Price: Around $2.50.
Who makes Sylvaner: Almadén, California Growers, Guglielmo, Gundlach-Bundschu, Hacienda, Hoffman, Mirassou, Monterey Vineyard, Sebastiani, a few others.

Vermouth
(Ver-MOOTH)

An appetizer wine, very good by itself "on the rocks," with a twist of lemon peel, or even mixed with soda. However, it is used most often in recent years as an ingredient in cocktails.

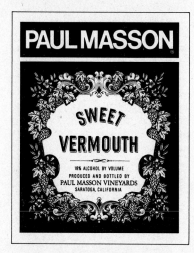

How it tastes: There are two kinds: dry and sweet (white and red, respectively). Dry vermouth is highly perfumed with herbs and spices; sweet vermouth also has flavorings added, but they are mellower and more robust.
How to serve: As indicated above. For cocktails, dry vermouth is added in small quantities (1 part in 6, or even less) to gin or vodka to make a martini. Sweet vermouth mixes in somewhat larger proportions (1 part in 3 or 4) with bourbon or Scotch whiskey to make a Manhattan or Rob Roy, respectively.
Price: $1.50 to $3.
Who makes vermouth: Nearly all the large-volume wineries in both California and New York.
Special note: Dry vermouth is a good seasoner for many foods. Several tablespoons may be added to a chicken or fish in braising or baking, for example.

Vidal Blanc
(Vee-doll BLAWN)

An excellent French-American hybrid grape for white wine. Plantings are being extended throughout the Midwest and East as the success of the wine becomes apparent.

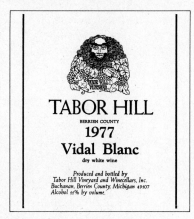

How it tastes: Crisp, dry, fruity, refreshing.
How to serve: With any fish, chicken, cold cuts, salmon loaf, luncheon fare. Also a good appetizer wine.
Price: Around $3.50.
Who makes Vidal Blanc: Indiana: Banholzer, Villa Medeo. Michigan: Bronte, St. Julian, Tabor Hill. Missouri: Mt. Pleasant, Stoltz. New York: Benmarl, Bully Hill. Ohio: Sublette, Valley Vineyards. Pennsylvania: Penn Shore, others.

Vignoles (Ravat 51)
(Veen-yole)(Rah-VAHT)

Here's an instance where the original name of a French hybrid grape may have been better than the new one. People can pronounce the original "Ravat" more easily than Vignoles, which most wineries are now using.
Vignoles has Chardonnay parentage, so the light-bodied white wine it makes could be a more authentic chablis than most of the generic American wines produced under that name. In France, Chardonnay grapes go into the true Chablis wines; our blended chablis rarely contains any Chardonnay because it's too expensive. Vignoles could provide a good compromise in this country.

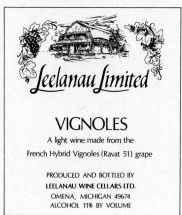

How it tastes: Vignoles is a dry, crisp white wine that makes an excellent appetizer.
How to serve: This wine suits all kinds of fish—baked, broiled, fried; it is also good with ham, eggs, sausage, and moderately spicy dishes.
Price: $3 to $4.
Who makes Vignoles: New York: Benmarl. New Jersey: Antuzzi's. Michigan: Boskydel and Leelanau. Maryland: Ziem Vineyards.

White Riesling

(White REEZ-ling)

This is the correct varietal name for the grape that in Germany produces the marvelous white wines of the Rhine and Mosel River districts. In California and certain other states, White Riesling grapes thrive and are used to make excellent wines—but under two different names. Some wineries call it Johannisberg Riesling; others, White Riesling. See a complete description on page 36, and a more general discussion of the Riesling grape family on page 30.

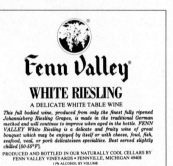

Fenn Valley®

WHITE RIESLING

A DELICATE WHITE TABLE WINE

This full bodied wine, produced from only the finest fully ripened Johannisberg Riesling Grapes, is made in the traditional German method and will continue to improve when aged in the bottle. FENN VALLEY White Riesling is a delicate and fruity wine of great bouquet which may be enjoyed by itself or with cheese, fowl, fish, seafood, veal, or pork delicatessen specialties. Best served slightly chilled (50-55°F).

PRODUCED AND BOTTLED IN OUR NATURALLY COOL CELLARS BY
FENN VALLEY VINEYARDS • FENNVILLE, MICHIGAN 49408
11% ALCOHOL BY VOLUME

White Riesling wine varies considerably, depending upon the growing conditions in the vineyard and the goal the winemaster had in mind. Because this grape is grown commercially in the Far West, Midwest, and East, you may want to sample bottles of White Riesling from various wineries in different states.

Zinfandel

(ZIN-fan-dell)

California's own red wine grapes produce a distinctive wine that may be made in at least three ways: as a fresh, young wine; as a wine to be aged several years to acquire complexity of flavor; and as a late-harvest wine, rich in alcohol (15 to 17 percent), which is not a mealtime wine, but a special wine to enjoy by itself.

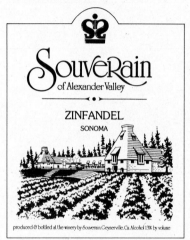

SouveRain
of Alexander Valley

ZINFANDEL
SONOMA

produced & bottled at the winery by Souverain, Geyserville, Ca. Alcohol 13% by volume

How it tastes: Young and fruity, dry, with a berry-like aroma and flavor. If aged, the bouquet is complex and suggests black currants, pepper, herbs, and spices.

How to serve: With roasts and chops, lamb dishes, all kinds of cheeses. A versatile wine.

Price: Ranges widely, from $2 to $4.50 for most. The special high-alcohol Zinfandels are limited in production and are quite expensive.

Who makes Zinfandel: Nearly 150 wineries in California, Washington, and Oregon. Generally available throughout the country from: Almadén, Paul Masson, Inglenook, Christian Brothers. Many small wineries

specialize in this wine, but they have produced limited bottlings thus far.

Special note: Although Zinfandel is a red grape, it has also been used to make white and rosé wines in recent years. The rosés, in particular, are worth trying for their delightful freshness, sometimes with even a hint of sparkle (fizz).

Other American Wines

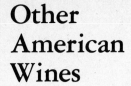

Even in the A-to-Z chapter, just concluded, it's impossible to list all the American wines you might come across in a wine shop. Some wines, as previously mentioned (page nine), are *proprietary*—that is, they carry trade names belonging to just one winery. In addition, a few of the unlisted varietal wines are still fairly rare, perhaps produced by only a few wineries. Still others have names that are slightly different from the ones listed in this chapter.

So for these and other reasons, the chapter is not absolutely complete. However, here in brief are some additional U.S. wine names you may encounter:

Chancellor. A deep red, high-quality hybrid grape and wine being produced in increasing quantities in the Midwest and East. Dry and full bodied in the style of Cabernet Sauvignon, it shows promise of becoming another elegant American red wine.

Claret. This generic label is applied less commonly to red wines than is burgundy (see page 13). The name claret is expected to disappear from general use in this country.

Flora. A hybrid white grape and its wine; it's based on Gewürztraminer stock. Total production is small and its future uncertain, even though the wine is quite "flowery" and pleasant.

Folle Blanche. A light, crisp white wine that's also in modest production in California. It probably will benefit from the increasing popularity of dry white wines generally.

Labrusca. This is the last part of the botanical name for our native American grape (*vitis labrusca*). Some Eastern wineries make a labrusca that's quite "grapey" in flavor and often has a bit of fizz to it.

Madeira. In this country, the name Madeira is applied to a heavy, sweet, fortified wine that bears little resemblance to the Portuguese original.

May Wine. A few wineries make a semisweet appetizer wine of light body under this name.

Pinot Saint George. This red varietal wine is bottled only by Christian Brothers, although other wineries have produced it at various times in the past.

Tokay. Another heavy, sweet, fortified wine similar to Madeira but based on an original Hungarian wine.

White Burgundy. A few wineries make a white version of their generic "burgundy," but it has no more specific meaning in this country than the red. White burgundy usually is of higher quality than red in the United States, however.

How Wine
Is Made

The Vines

Grapevines are planted from cuttings rather than seed. This ensures a new plant that's true to its "parent" in all important ways. (Sometimes cuttings of one type of grape are grafted to the hardier rootstocks of another type.) Newly rooted cuttings then spend their first year in a nursery before emerging to begin yet another vineyard.

It takes four or five years for a grapevine to begin bearing a commercial crop of wine grapes. Once started in production, however, a vine may bear for 25 or even as many as 50 years.

Early in each new year, before buds and shoots appear, the vines must be pruned back severely (left). This channels the plant's energy into its fruit rather than into excessive leaves and stems. But that's not the last concern facing the grower. Spring frosts are a perennial problem in many areas, followed by rain at the wrong time; too little or too much sunshine; too much heat or cold; and various insect, bird, animal, and fungus pests.

Most vineyards provide a trellis support for the vines (right), to enhance their exposure to the sun as well as to simplify harvesting. What you see above ground is only a fraction of the vine; its root system extends many feet into the ground. So long as the water table doesn't fail them, grapevines can survive one or more years of drought.

Despite all these hazards, there is nearly always a harvest—and in California especially, the climate is moderate enough to make it a predictably good one for most varieties of grapes. Other parts of the U.S. have more uncertainties of climate, but new hybrid vines are improving harvests rapidly.

How Wine
Is Made

The Grapes

Grapes ripen between late August and early October, depending upon the grape variety, the section of the country, and the weather conditions prevailing in the vineyard. Traditionally, grapes were picked by hand, but today there are mechanical pickers that can do the job if the vines are properly spaced and trellised and do not grow on steep slopes.

Heavy rains at harvesttime can ruin the quality of the wine by causing it to become thin and watery. Late or early frosts can limit or greatly damage the crop. And grapes have a variety of predators, including birds, bees, rabbits, and deer. The grower's worries aren't over until he's delivered grapes to the winery.

As a rule, grape varieties that produce abundant clusters of grapes turn out to be rather bland when made into wine. Such grapes, typically, grow best in hot areas such as California's Central Valley. Conversely, vines that bear sparingly often concentrate their flavor and thus are more highly valued for wine making. They grow best on slopes and atop ridges, like those found in California's coastal counties and in New York State's Finger Lakes district.

It's important to harvest the grapes when their sugar content indicates satisfactory ripeness. However, some "late harvest" wines are made from grapes richer than normal in sugar—and thus richer and sweeter in flavor as well.

Other important characteristics of wine grapes are their acid content (which should be in balance with the sugar) and the amount of tannin (the astringent, mouth-puckering quality of certain red wines).

How Wine
Is Made

NOTICE

All grapes being delivered to the winery
for the account of Allied Grape Growers
will be received in accordance with
United Vintners 1976 Quality Standards.
Any load of grapes which is determined
to be Grade 'B' or 'C' according to these
Quality Standards may be withdrawn.

Harvesting

Autumn harvest in the wine country brings hectic, round-the-clock work to everyone connected with a winery. Grapes flood in aboard unceasing convoys of trucks, and they must be processed as quickly as possible to safeguard the quality of the wine-to-be.

Some wineries grow their own grapes; others buy on the open market or from suppliers with whom they've contracted in advance. As in this view of New York's Finger Lakes district (right), the grapes arrive in open containers sized to fit the winery's handling equipment.

First stop is a stemmer-crusher like the California version shown at left. Revolving paddles inside perforated metal cylinders knock the grapes from their stems and break their skins. Stems, leaves, and other debris are removed; the "crush," as it's now called, moves on to a press. Here, the grapes are gently squeezed to extract more juice without breaking the seeds, which might otherwise impart an unpleasant taste.

Nearly all wine grape juice is colorless, regardless of the grape's skin color. If white wine is made from grapes with colored skins, all seeds and skins are removed after pressing. Rosé wines stay mixed with solid materials for a matter of hours to a day or so; red wines keep company with their seeds and skins until after fermentation is complete.

Obviously, white grapes will make only white wine. But red grapes can produce white, rosé, or red wines, depending upon how they are handled in the winery. Red wines also pick up tannin and other substances from their seeds and skins; this is why reds are usually more complex in flavor and aroma.

How Wine
Is Made

Fermentation

Although there are natural yeasts present on the grape skins, natural fermentation is unpredictable and difficult to control. Therefore, the crush is given a light dose of sulfur dioxide to inhibit bacterial growth, and a special yeast culture is added. The crush or "must," as it is called, is ready for fermentation.

Wines can be fermented in all sorts of containers, from small barrels to concrete vats; but many wineries use temperature-controlled stainless steel fermenters (left, above). Because fermentation causes heat, it's important to keep the must at the proper temperature—particularly if it is a white wine—so it won't lose its fresh flavor.

White wines are fermented cold, at about 55 degrees (Fahrenheit); red wines are fermented at about 80 degrees. For dry wines, the fermentation goes on until all of the grape sugar is converted into alcohol, which may take as long as two weeks. For sweet wines, the fermentation can be stopped by chilling when there is still sugar in the wine.

After fermentation, both red and white wines are "racked" (siphoned) into a variety of containers. These are sometimes wood (right), such as redwood or oak, which soften or round out the flavors of red wines in particular. Many white wines are kept only in stainless steel or glass-lined tanks to "keep their fruit"—preserve fresh flavor.

An important part of any winery is the laboratory (left, below), where samples of wines at all stages of development are analyzed. Careful quality control ensures that wine leaves a modern winery in good condition on its way to the consumer.

How Wine
Is Made

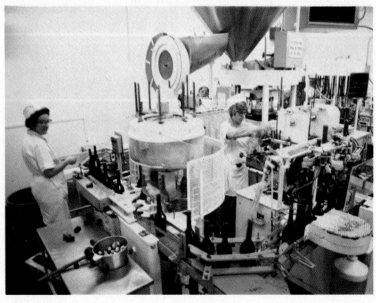

Aging

A lot happens to a wine after fermentation but before bottling. Racking (left) may be necessary several times to remove dead yeasts and other sediment. Each tank must then be "topped" with wine to replace the lost material. This additional wine may come from the same vintage or possibly an older vintage of the same wine.

Sometimes wines are clear and bright after racking, but usually it's necessary to filter, "cold stabilize" (chill to precipitate tartrates), or centrifuge (spin) them to eliminate any remaining sediment. The treatment needed varies with individual wines. Although sediment is harmless, it doesn't look pretty in the glass.

Before wine is bottled, "fining" may be required. This process removes the very fine materials that might cause the wine to look slightly hazy; it's not always done, but it is common. Fining materials include egg white, gelatin, and bentonite—all natural adhesives that gather up very small particles in wine and are themselves removed after their job is done.

Some wines are aged before fining in small oak casks (right). This process smooths out their flavors and imparts just the right amount of "woodiness" to certain wines such as Cabernet Sauvignon and Chardonnay—our finest red and white wines, respectively. A final "polishing" filtration sometimes is given before the wine is at last ready for bottling.

Finished wines may be bottled (left), corked, capped, labeled, and packed in containers for storage or shipping—all in one continuous process in modern wineries. This step is usually shown to visitors on tours prior to wine tasting.

How Wine
Is Made

Tasting

For certain members of every winery, tasting is both a joy and a job. Laboratory technicians (page 52) can chemically analyze a wine with great precision, but only the educated palate of the winemaker (right) can judge whether a particular wine will be pleasing—or will even someday be truly outstanding.

Samples of every batch are tasted regularly throughout the wine making process. Careful records are kept on dozens of wine characteristics—and eventually a "personality profile" emerges which the winemaster can evaluate. Some wines turn out so well they can be released after aging in cask or bottle. Other wines, however, call for blending to meet the winery's own standards.

Blending can work in several ways. Sometimes different batches of the same kind of wine are mixed to bolster strong points and overcome weaknesses in each one. Sometimes wines from different years are blended for similar reasons. Frequently wine from one varietal grape (such as Cabernet Sauvignon) is blended with another varietal (such as Merlot) to improve color or flavors. For varietal wines, a 1978 federal regulation will soon require that 75 percent be made from grapes named on the label—but the other 25 percent may be blended from several different kinds of grapes, if the winemaster chooses.

Another kind of wine tasting also takes place at many wineries (left). Here, individuals and groups of visitors get a chance to sample the specialties of the house—and to buy if they wish. Tours are frequently offered in conjunction with the tasting rooms; see page 92 for more information.

Special Kinds of Wine

Most wines consumed in this country are "table wines," containing 11 to 14 percent alcohol and meant to be served with meals. There are other wines to consider, however. On this page is a discussion of the higher-alcohol wines intended for use before or after a meal. On page 60 is a review of sparkling wines like champagne, which are served on various special occasions.

Appetizer and Dessert Wines

In keeping with the informality of most life-styles today, Americans no longer observe rigid rules about which wines to serve before and after meals. However, there are categories of "fortified" wines, containing 17 to 20 percent alcohol, which have traditionally been described as either appetizer ("aperitif") or dessert wines.

Fortified wines first go through normal fermentation; this would provide an alcohol content of no more than 14 percent because the yeasts are killed at or before this concentration. Additional alcohol—usually in the form of brandy—is provided by the winemaster. Sometimes such fortification takes place before the fermentation is complete, thereby leaving some unfermented sugar (and a sweet taste) in the wine. Such sweet, fortified wines are commonly called "dessert wines." If brandy is added after all the sugar in the wine has fermented into alcohol, the result is a relatively dry, higher-alcohol wine that is appropriate as an appetizer.

Sherry. This is our most popular fortified wine—and it's made either dry or sweet. Dry sherries carry label designations such as "dry sherry," "flor sherry," or "cocktail sherry." Sweet sherries are usually called "golden sherry" or "cream sherry," although there's no cream involved. An example of American cream sherry, in an unusual bottle by Paul Masson, is pictured at right.

Some U.S. wineries—including Almadén, Beaulieu, Concannon, Louis M. Martini, and Sebastiani in California—use the outdoor stacked-cask "solera" method of producing their sherries (see page 42). An oxidation takes place as the wine is warmed naturally by the sun or by heating it in tanks to about 110 degrees (Fahrenheit). This heating speeds up the aging process, changes the flavor, and produces a distinctive amber color—pale in dry sherry, deeper in sweet sherry.

Port. This is our most commonly served fortified dessert wine. Like sherry, it can be made in a variety of styles. There is a red "ruby port"; an amber "tawny port"; and a relatively light-hued "white port." All are sweet, but their sweetness and flavor vary considerably within types and from one winery to another.

Vermouth. Probably used more as a cocktail mixer than as a sipping wine in this country, vermouth is both fortified and flavored with aromatic herbs (see page 43). Dry (white) vermouth can be served chilled or "on the rocks" as an appetizer wine; sweet (red) vermouth is occasionally served at room temperature as a dessert wine.

Other Fortified Wines

Several other higher-alcohol wines produced in this country seldom measure up in quality to the ones described above. For example, a few American wineries make a *madeira* dessert wine that bears little resemblance to the famous Portuguese wine of that name. The same is true of our *tokay*, which doesn't even begin with the same grapes used in Hungary to make the original Tokaj wine.

Our *muscatel* wine is a strictly native American invention based on Muscat grapes, but it tastes more like the essence of raisins than anything else. Finally, there are proprietary (private label) wines such as Gallo's Thunderbird and Mogen David's 20-20 that fit the legal definition of fortified wines.

Special Kinds of Wine

How Champagne Is Made

There are two ways to make champagne. The traditional French *méthode champenoise* takes much time and care; the newer *Charmat* (SHAR-mah) bulk process is a shortcut used for less expensive champagnes and other sparkling wines. It was invented by a Frenchman named Charmat, but interestingly enough it's forbidden in France's Champagne district.

In either case, the winery begins by fermenting a basic, rather neutral-flavored white wine. A second fermentation, brought about by the addition of sugar and a special yeast, creates the familiar carbon dioxide bubbles. The second fermentation takes place within the champagne bottle itself in the *méthode champenoise*, and inside large sealed tanks in the *Charmat* process.

Yeast sediment forms during this fermentation, of course. To get rid of it in the traditional process, a great deal of hand turning of inverted bottles is required over a span of many months. The sediment collects in the necks and is removed in a final bottle-by-bottle "disgorging" step. Some wineries now substitute a "transfer" step at the very end of their process. In this case, an entire batch of champagne is emptied mechanically from individual bottles, then filtered and rebottled under pressure.

In France, only sparkling wines made in the Champagne district may use that name. The U.S. permits the label "champagne" to be applied to sparkling wines made by either of the processes described here—but "Charmat" or "Bulk Process" must appear on the labels of bottles produced in that manner.

Producers in California making sparkling wine of high quality, such as Schramsberg, Korbel, Hanns Kornell, Mirassou, and Domaine Chandon (a French company), all use the *méthode champenoise*. The Christian Brothers employ the *Charmat* process for a popular-priced champagne. Almadén has two lines of champagne and uses the "transfer" technique in one of them. Other producers make most of their champagnes with the *Charmat* method.

The finest California champagnes are made with classic French grapes—Chardonnay and Pinot Noir. The *Charmat* process requires only good basic white wine of no special grape pedigree.

In the East, large companies such as Taylor and Great Western ferment Aurora, Delaware, and other medium-quality grapes. Gold Seal has enough Chardonnay growing in the Finger Lakes district to be able to use that grape for its Charles Fournier champagne label.

Other Sparkling Wines

Inexpensive red wine grapes are also used in the tank-fermented *Charmat* process to make sparkling burgundy like the one shown at right. Its quality and price are usually lower than champagne's, but a well-chilled bottle can be appropriate at a midsummer picnic.

Pink champagne originates as a rosé wine and goes through the steps outlined previously. Cold duck (see page 21) is a mixture of red and white sparkling wines.

So-called crackling wines owe their bubbles (which are fewer than in champagne or sparkling burgundy) to various other processes. Technically, they are not true sparkling wines.

Wine—How to Buy, Care for, and Serve

Shopping for Wine

Fortune smiles on you if in your town it is possible to buy wine in the supermarket or at a retail wine shop. Regulations vary, however, and wine buying in a few states still is subject to the whims of a liquor control board that denies you a full range of choice.

In a growing number of states and cities, however, wine may be purchased as easily as foods for family meals—a logical and convenient procedure. It has also brought women into wine selection, which once was held to be the right and privilege of men alone.

A good retail wine shop may carry a wide range of wines and quite possibly specialize in some of California's famous vintages. In addition, a good wine shop is almost always operated by an informed, helpful person who cares about wines and is happy to share knowledge with customers. The shop may have its own wine club, offering tastings, seminars, and special sales. Through such an organization, you will meet others who love wine—some of whom may become good friends. As a French proverb tells us, "In water one sees one's own face, but in wine

one beholds the heart of another."

Be wary of buying wine in a store that displays its bottles standing up, unless you are sure the stock sells quickly. Only a wet cork protects wine. A dry one, which may result from the bottle's being in an upright position for months, can shrink and let air into the wine, thus spoiling it.

Don't buy a bottle from a shop window, either. Heat and light are wine's enemies, whether the source is the sun or an electric sign.

If you have a wide choice of wines and wineries, take advantage of the good luck. Buy the same wine under different labels, and buy different wines from a favorite winery. And al-ways expand your tastes. Move on from generic "burgundy" and "chablis" to varietal wines. French Colombard is very different from Gewürztraminer; Petite Sirah, easily recognizable after you've tried it a few times, bears little resemblance to Zinfandel. Even the taste of Zinfandel, say, depends upon such factors as where the grapes were grown and how the winemaker chose to make the wine.

Three Basic Wines

George Washington once wrote, "My manner of living is plain. A glass of wine and a piece of mutton are always ready, and such as are content to partake of that are always welcome." It's still good to have something ready for a visitor, though today the food accompanying the wine would probably be fruit or cheese instead of mutton.

Serving wine can truly become an adventure—but you do have to start somewhere. Certainly, a basic wine stock could consist of just three bottles: a cocktail sherry, a dry white table wine, and a dry red. The white wine could be a generic type like chablis, or a varietal like a California

Wine—How to Buy, Care for, and Serve

Chenin Blanc; the red might be a burgundy or "mountain red," or a varietal Ruby Cabernet or inexpensive Zinfandel. Any of these may be bought in a large economy size, 1.5 liters (50.7 ounces), for example.

Keep in mind, though, that these big containers of wine need refrigeration after they've been opened, with the exception of sherry. (But refrigerate the sherry, too, because it tastes better chilled.) However, not every family has a refrigerator large enough to accommodate big bottles of wine, as well as large containers of milk and orange juice.

There's another problem with red wine in large containers. If you keep a partly used bottle in the refrigerator, bring the wine out soon enough to reach cool room temperature before drinking it. On the other hand, alternate chilling and warming aren't very good for any wine. One answer: buy red wine in an even larger size—three liters, perhaps—and divide it into four 750-milliliter bottles, each well corked, to be used at various times as needed. Be sure the bottles are sparkling clean, and keep the wine cool, if not refrigerated.

If you decide to hurry the warming of a chilled bottle of red wine by immersing it in warm water, as if it were a baby's bottle of milk, don't let anyone see you do it! That's a *no-no*, though it probably would not hurt a sturdy, inexpensive red wine.

Quality wines, such as California Chardonnay and Cabernet Sauvignon, require more care. If you wish to keep them on hand instead of buying them as you need them, give some thought to a wine cellar.

Planning a Wine Cellar

Perhaps some day you'd like to collect fine wines and keep them a year or more to mature. If so, you'll need a storage room that is dark, cool (55 to 60 degrees Fahrenheit), well ventilated, fairly dry, and free from vibrations that might cause the wine to mature more rapidly than it should.

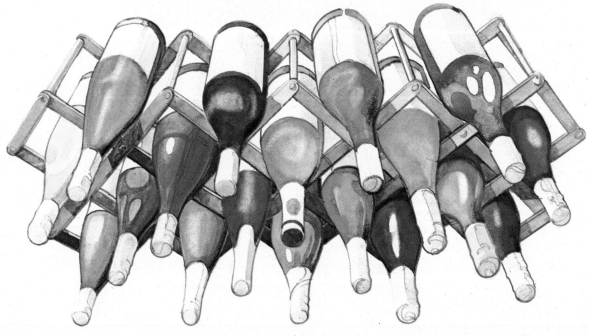

A root cellar or storage room for canned goods, which older homes sometimes provide, makes a good cellar for wines so long as it isn't near the furnace. The wine hobbyist who can afford to do so sometimes air-conditions a little-used bedroom or den, then builds in shelves or bins for wine. Another alternative is to buy a ready-made storage unit, with racks for wines and controlled temperature—a handsome object that looks like a piece of furniture.

Some of these options are expensive. Many families can't afford a wine cellar and the wine stock to fill it—nor do they have the space. But sometimes a cool spot may be found under a stairway or in a closet, where a few favorite wines may be stored on their sides for a few months at least. If you're handy at carpentry, you may be able to build racks into a cupboard that isn't near a heating pipe or radiator.

How Much Wine?

A 750-milliliter (close in size to the old "fifth") bottle of wine usually serves three or four at a family-style dinner. You might want to splurge on a weekend and buy two bottles, or one of the larger 1.5-liter size.

For entertaining, plan on one bottle for every two persons. That, in fact, is a good guide for banquets and wine tastings: count noses and add up a half bottle per person. Some may drink more than that; others will usually drink less.

If by chance you are inviting people who are genuine wine buffs and if the wine is particularly good, you'd better count noses and add up one bottle for each nose! If it isn't all consumed, you can always enjoy it

yourself at another time.

Wine leftovers should be tightly corked and kept in the refrigerator. If a red wine will be finished in a day or two, it may be left out in a cool room, which will give it the best temperature for drinking.

Leftover wine may also be used in cooking, of course.

Cooking with Wine

Wine adds pleasing flavor to many kinds of food. But don't overdo a good thing. If you look for subtlety in a sauce, don't replace more than two tablespoons per cup of liquid with wine, unless you've tried the dish before and know you can use more wine without harming the dish.

For example, if you're making two cups of a chicken stock and cream sauce for chicken or seafood, you probably could replace ¼ cup (four tablespoons) of the stock with a dry white wine or a dry sherry, leaving the cream at its prescribed measure. Similarly, for two cups of a white sauce, you'd substitute ¼ cup of the wine for an equal measure of milk. Red wine should never be used in any white sauce—the result may be a dirty gray sauce.

In a stew, you might be more generous with wine. Because most stews are not meant to have delicate or restrained flavor, a cup of red wine in a pot of stew for a family of six will not be too much.

Wine can also add flavor to many soups. Sherry is first choice for a fish or chicken soup, but dry white wine may go into any cream soup—it is particularly delicious in vichyssoise or a seafood bisque.

Sweet wines, such as those suggested for dessert on page 58, may be poured over a com-

bination of fruits to be served for dessert. Or substitute them for part of the liquid in a bread pudding. Use them also to saturate the pieces of cake or ladyfingers in a trifle.

What about leftover wine from a party? An inventive cook never has a problem using it up, unless that person must also compete with a family of eager wine drinkers!

Appreciating Wine

You don't have to be obvious about it, but to get the most from a glass of wine, you need to follow several steps. Look around a good restaurant and you'll notice that even a wine expert is very likely doing the same things.

First, look at the wine to admire its brilliance and color. At home, hold the glass to the light or against a white tablecloth. If the wine is cloudy or faded, too bad!

Next, smell the wine. Don't be shy. Get your nose into the glass. This is the crucial test—if the wine smells good, it will taste good. If it is a red wine or fragrant white, swirl it about in the glass (this is one reason for not filling the glass too close to the top) to catch all the nuances of its bouquet. Finally, of course, begin to drink the wine.

It would be ridiculous to make a lot of fuss over a simple three-dollar wine you know will be good but not great. Nevertheless, the look-smell-taste process is an automatic response with most wine drinkers, and it usually takes only a few seconds, with no one else the wiser. It serves to eliminate a bad wine—and there *are* wines that have been badly made or kept too long or poorly. It also adds to the enjoyment of a really good wine.

Wine—How to Buy Care for, and Serve

Restaurant Wine Lists

Buying a bottle of wine in a wine shop is easier for most people than choosing one from a restaurant wine list. All too many fine restaurants still assume that imported is always better, and you are faced with a long column of French names with eye-popping prices after them. Skipping over the shorter German and Italian listings, you may come upon the names of unfamiliar California "boutique" (small winery) wines, also with whopping price tags—sometimes as much as $25 or $30 a bottle for a Cabernet Sauvignon in a good vintage.

This can be a dismaying experience. Can the dinner wine possibly cost more than the dinner? Yes, it can, but it shouldn't.

What do you do, faced with such a wine list? You simply ask for a glass or carafe of the restaurant's "house wine" and make a mental note to bring more money next time or avoid the restaurant altogether.

A house wine should not cost more than a cocktail, by the glass. It should really cost less, but unfortunately, it seldom does.

A French restaurant's house wines will almost always be French—often a Macon Blanc for a white wine, and a Bordeaux Superieur for the red. A French rosé wine may be from Provence or the Loire; Rosé d'Anjou is often the selection. These are all good basic wines, although their prices have become inflated in recent years. The restaurant may regard this as justification for charging $1.50 for a glass.

In an Italian restaurant, you may fare better. There are many moderately priced wines, and a bottle may not be too costly.

The house wine is likely to be a Soave for white and Valpolicella for red.

These two wines are light and agreeable. You might like one of them as an appetizer, by the glass, and then choose a bottle of fuller-bodied, stronger-flavored red wine such as a Chianti Classico or Barolo to follow with the dinner.

You will rarely, if ever, find a German wine sold by the glass as a house wine. If you want a German wine and don't understand the names on the wine list, ask the waiter to help you. He will be flattered, and may be knowledgeable enough to introduce you to a better wine than the common white Liebfraumilch or Zeller Schwarzkatz. But in a pinch, order either of those. Incidentally, nearly all German wines are white, and the best of them are Rieslings.

In small, inexpensive restaurants and in the dining rooms of popular hotels and motels, you will probably find a brief wine list dominated by a single American winery—Paul Masson, The Christian Brothers, or Almaden. In most instances, the salesman from the wine company has set up the list. It is easy for the restaurateur and gives most customers no problem. Usually you can buy a bottle, half bottle, carafe, or glass.

As we mentioned elsewhere, white wines generally go best with lighter foods such as seafood, fowl, veal dishes, and the like. Red wines complement heartier fare such as steaks, roasts, and spicy ethnic dishes. Rosés—especially good varietal ones—go with most anything on the menu. Sparkling wines usually are ordered on special occasions and are consumed in place of cocktails. Remember that you may end up ordering more than one bottle of wine, thus adding to your total bill.

Be aware that sometimes U.S. restaurants don't take the best care of wine. Especially when served by the glass, wine can show loss of quality if the bottle has been open too long. If this happens to you, don't hesitate to reject the wine. The waiter should open a fresh bottle and pour a replacement.

A few restaurants permit you to bring your own wine. Then they may charge a "corkage" fee. They are entitled to do this because of the service involved. They may have to chill a wine for you as well as open and serve it, and of course, they do furnish the glasses.

An expensive restaurant with a lengthy wine list almost never permits anyone to bring in their own wine.

How much should you be expected to pay for a bottle of wine to go with your restaurant meal? There are no limits, unfortunately, and many restaurants charge too much. Twice the restaurant's cost would not be out of line, for the restaurant must care for the wine—and that means, often enough, maintaining a temperature- and humidity-controlled wine cellar. Perhaps your best plan is to decide in advance how much you can afford for your bottle with dinner—and then see if you can

spot an "old friend" at that price on the restaurant's list.

An encouraging sign is a growing tendency on the part of large and prestigious restaurants to include a long list of California wines at a wide range of prices, so that no customer need be intimidated. In New York, for example, the famous Windows on the World restaurant has a list of 90 wines from 14 countries, with 30 wines priced at $7.50 or less. In Chicago, the Ritz-Carlton Hotel lists a number of California wines at less than $10 a bottle.

In California's large cities, as might be expected, some of the restaurant wine lists are delightful, with something for every taste and pocketbook.

We're a long way from 50-cents-a-glass restaurant wine, which might be the ideal, but at least some very fine restaurants are aware that sky-high wine prices frighten away customers, and they are doing something about it.

Opening, Pouring Wine

Most wines may simply be opened and poured. They don't

need to "breathe," and they don't need decanting (pouring into a fancy container). All you require are a good corkscrew and shiningly clean, detergent-free glasses. Red wines should be served at "cool room temperature" (around 65 degrees Fahrenheit), while white wines should be somewhat colder (around 50 degrees is ideal). Fifteen to 20 minutes in an ice bucket or about an hour in your refrigerator will chill a white wine properly. But don't over-chill or you'll kill the bouquet and, therefore, much of the taste—the sense of smell accounts for about 90 percent of the taste sensation.

Work with a good corkscrew when you open a bottle of wine. There are many kinds, but the two most popular are the simple, flat one every wine waiter carries around in a pocket, and the auger type with wings that act as levers. The latter is easy to use, but unless you're careful, it can chew up a weak cork. The wine waiter's corkscrew has an open spiral that won't damage the cork.

Keep several different corkscrews on hand, so that if you have difficulty with one, you can switch to another type. As you may have guessed, many wine buffs collect corkscrews.

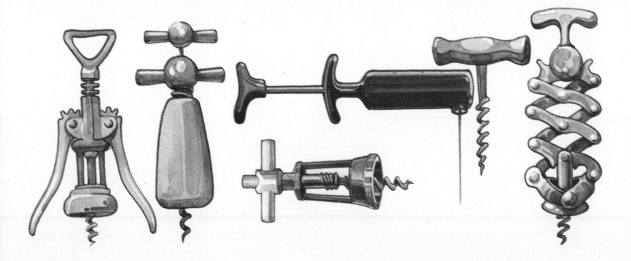

Wine—How to Buy, Care for, and Serve

The Right Glasses

A few years ago, before there were so many wine lovers around, it was hard to find a decent glass in which to serve wine. Most of them were too small, of ugly shape, and even of colored glass. That last problem was the worst, because how could people admire the golden or rosy or amber or ruby tones of wine through "rose colored glasses"? They'd get false impressions.

Nowadays, there are all kinds of glasses—many of them far too big; many others, beautiful and graceful but far too expensive. There are glasses of tulip shape, flute shape, thistle shape, and big round goblets that look impressive on the table but won't fit your dishwasher.

It's a relief to know that just one set of well-shaped, fairly long-stemmed "tulip" glasses (nine or ten ounces in size) will do for any wine, even champagne and sherry. Of course, if you can afford—and can find room for—another set of glasses, it's nice to have smaller containers for sherry and sweet dessert wines. Sweet wines should be served in smaller portions than dry table wines, and everyone has a tendency to pour too much into a large glass. And because most dessert wines have more alcohol than other wines, they shouldn't be poured too generously.

Wineglasses are among your more fragile possessions. Since the thinnest glass usually costs the most, too, you're wise to settle for something a bit sturdier so you won't be so concerned about breakage.

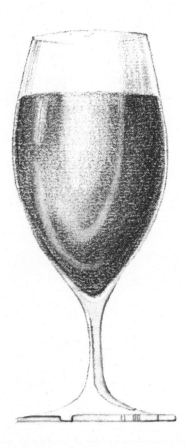

Wine Tastings

One of the best ways to improve your judgment and appreciation of wine is to invite friends over for a wine tasting session. This needn't be a pretentious occasion—but it shouldn't have an unrestrained, cocktail-party atmosphere, either. To learn more about wine, you do need reasonably clear heads, along with a step-by-step tasting procedure.

You're wise to limit the scope of the tasting. Establish a theme. You could match up inexpensive red or white "jug" wines, for example, or rate a group of varietal rosés, or compare White Rieslings from various sections of California as well as Washington state, the Midwest, and the East. You might go through the A-to-Z section in this book and pick out wines that are unfamiliar but sound intriguing, and look for similarities and differences among them as you taste.

Serve red wines at cool room temperature, and chill the whites. Try to assemble enough extra (and *clean*) glasses so tasters won't have to rinse between wines. Provide good lighting and a white background, if possible, for judging wine color.

Six to eight wines are about all a nonprofessional group can evaluate at one sitting. Prepare a chart for each taster that allows separate scores for *appearance, aroma, body,* and *flavor*—with a range of zero to five points per category. Theoretically, a perfect wine would then rate 20 points (five points in each of the four categories), while an average, acceptable wine might score in the 13 to 15 point range.

The order of tasting should be dry before sweet, white before red, and light-bodied before full-bodied. Provide dishes of plain, low-salt crackers (no strong flavors to compete with the wines); slices of mild cheese are all right for informal groups.

"Blind" tastings can be fun, and perhaps more accurate because they tend to eliminate prejudices. All labels are covered, and each wine is identified only by number until tasting is complete.

GOOD MATCHES OF FOOD AND WINE

Appetizers	Cheese dips, spicy or oniony snacks, antipasto, raw vegetables with dip	Dry *flor* sherry, cocktail sherry (not cream sherry)
	Raw oysters, clams	Chardonnay, French Colombard, Seyval Blanc, Pinot Blanc
Cold Buffet Foods	Sliced turkey, ham, beef, summer sausage, salads, breads, cheese	Dry rosé wines, Gamay, Gamay Noir, Pinot Noir, Baco Noir, Gewürztraminer
Fish and Seafood	Baked or fried fillets	Chenin Blanc, Emerald Riesling, French Colombard, dry Sauvignon Blanc, Sylvaner, Vidal Blanc
	Baked fresh salmon, poached salmon, trout, or whitefish	Chardonnay, White Riesling, Seyval Blanc; Gamay or Merlot (for salmon)
	Fish or seafood with a rich sauce	Chardonnay, Gewürztraminer
	Shrimp, crab, or lobster, (steamed, broiled, hot or cold, plain)	Chenin Blanc, Fumé Blanc, Sauvignon Blanc, Chardonnay, White Riesling, Seyval Blanc
	Shrimp (barbecued, creole, jambalaya), other seafood with spicy sauce, seafood salad	Rosé of Pinot Noir, Grignolino or Zinfandel, Chardonnay, Gewürztraminer Barbera, Foch
Meats, Game, Poultry	Beef (roast, hot or cold, steaks)	Cabernet Sauvignon, Pinot Noir, Petite Sirah, aged Baco Noir, Chancellor
	Beef (pot roast)	Chelois, Ruby Cabernet, Zinfandel
	Barbecued beef	Baco Noir, Petite Sirah, Zinfandel
	Veal (roast)	Chenin Blanc, Sauvignon Blanc, White Riesling, Cabernet Sauvignon, Zinfandel
	Lamb (roast, chops)	Baco Noir, Cabernet Sauvignon, aged Foch, Merlot, Petite Sirah, Zinfandel

Meats, Game, Poultry *continued*	Pork (roast, chops)	Chenin Blanc, Gewürztraminer, Barbera, Cabernet Sauvignon, De Chaunac, Gamay, Gamay Beaujolais
	Ham	Still or sparkling rosé, Chenin Blanc, Dutchess, Gamay Beaujolais, Gewürztraminer (for Virginia-style ham)
	Venison (roast, chops)	Cabernet Sauvignon, Petite Sirah, Pinot Noir, Baco Noir, Chancellor, Chelois, De Chaunac
	Chicken, turkey	Chenin Blanc, Fumé Blanc, Sauvignon Blanc, Pinot Blanc, Vidal Blanc, Seyval Blanc, White Riesling, Emerald Riesling
	Barbecued chicken, turkey with spicy stuffing	Gewürztraminer, Barbera, Cabernet Sauvignon, Gamay, Gamay Beaujolais, Zinfandel
	Fried chicken, chicken salad	Chenin Blanc, dry Delaware, Gamay, Gamay Beaujolais
	Duck, goose	Chardonnay, Pinot Noir, Baco Noir, Chancellor
	Pheasant	Cabernet Sauvignon, Petite Sirah, Pinot Noir, Chancellor
Cheese	Blue, Camembert, Brie, Chevre	Baco Noir, Barbera, Chancellor, Petite Sirah, Cabernet Sauvignon, Pinot Noir, Chancellor, Foch, Zinfandel
	Cheddar	Baco Noir, Foch, Petite Sirah, Pinot Noir
Pasta	Spaghetti with meat sauce, lasagna, other Italian-style dishes	Barbera, Chelois, Foch
Dessert	Pastry, fruit (not citrus), fruit pies, tarts, fruitcake, pound cake, plain cookies	Aurora, Catawba, sweet Chenin Blanc, Late Harvest White Riesling, Semillon, Malvasia Bianca, Moscato di Canelli

Cooking with Wine

The recipes that follow suggest ideas on how to use wine in cooking. You'll find that wine imparts a unique flavor and aroma to a variety of foods, from entrées to desserts.

Generally, red wines are suggested for heartier recipes, while white wines are used in delicately flavored foods. However, you may want to try other combinations.

For cooking, select well-flavored wines that aren't too expensive. It's also a good way to use any leftover wine you may have.

Some suggested dry white wines include chablis, Emerald Riesling, dry Semillon, and Sylvaner. A few suggested dry red wines include burgundy, Chancellor, Chelois, Ruby Cabernet, and Zinfandel.

Ham Veronique is a tasty, easy recipe to prepare. Just quickly brown a ham slice, stir together a wine sauce, and simmer ham in the wine mixture. Add green grapes the last few minutes of cooking.

HAM VERONIQUE

Easy way to dress up a ham steak—

2 tablespoons butter
2 tablespoons sugar
  Dash ground ginger
1 2¼-pound fully cooked ham slice, cut 1½ inches thick
1 tablespoon chopped green onion
¾ cup dry red wine
1 tablespoon cornstarch
1 cup seedless green grapes

Melt butter in large skillet. Sprinkle in sugar and ginger. Brown ham quickly on both sides in mixture. Remove ham. Cook onion in drippings till tender. Blend in wine; cook and stir till boiling. Combine cornstarch and ¼ cup *cold water.* Add to wine mixture. Cook and stir till bubbly. Return ham to skillet; cover and cook over low heat for 15 minutes. Halve grapes. Add to ham; cook 1 to 2 minutes more. Spoon grapes and sauce over ham on warm platter. Serves 6.

CRANBERRY-WINE GLAZED HAM

Burgundy is a good choice for this—

1 10- to 14-pound bone-in fully cooked ham
  Whole cloves
1 16-ounce can whole cranberry sauce
1 cup packed brown sugar
½ cup dry red wine
2 teaspoons prepared mustard

Place ham, fat side up, into shallow roasting pan, Score fat into diamond pattern; stud with cloves. Insert meat thermometer. Bake in 325° oven for 3 to 3½ hours or till meat thermometer registers 140°. In saucepan stir together cranberry sauce, brown sugar, wine, and mustard; simmer, uncovered, 5 minutes. During last 30 minutes baking time for ham, spoon *half* of cranberry mixture over ham. Pass remaining cranberry mixture. Makes about 20 to 28 servings.

PORK CHOP SKILLET

A prize-winning skillet mixture—

2 tablespoons all-purpose flour
½ teaspoon salt
¼ teaspoon pepper
¼ teaspoon garlic powder
4 pork chops, cut ½ inch thick
      . . .
4 ounces salt pork, finely chopped (optional)
4 ounces bulk Italian sausage
1 medium green pepper, diced
1 medium onion, chopped (½ cup)
      . . .
1 cup dry white wine
½ teaspoon dried thyme, crushed
2 or 3 bay leaves
1 small cabbage, cut into 8 wedges
1 16-ounce can whole new potatoes, drained

Combine flour, salt, pepper, and garlic powder. Coat pork chops with flour mixture. In skillet brown salt pork till crisp. Add Italian sausage, green pepper, and onion; cook till sausage is browned. Remove from skillet; drain, reserving 1 tablespoon drippings.

Brown pork chops in reserved drippings; add sausage mixture, wine, thyme, and bay leaves. Arrange cabbage wedges atop. Simmer, covered, 20 to 25 minutes. Add drained potatoes; simmer, uncovered, 10 minutes longer or till hot. Makes 4 servings.

BOEUF EN CROUTE

Serve this on a special occasion–

¾ cup dry red wine
¾ cup dry sherry
1 onion, quartered
2 bay leaves
1 4-pound beef eye round roast
  Mushroom Filling
2 cups all-purpose flour
½ teaspoon salt
⅔ cup shortening
⅓ to ½ cup cold water
1 beaten egg
  Gravy

Combine wine, sherry, onion, and bay leaves. Place roast into heavy plastic bag; add wine mixture. Marinate roast overnight in refrigerator, turning bag occasionally to distribute marinade.

Prepare Mushroom Filling; cover and chill.

Remove meat from marinade, reserving marinade. Place meat on rack in shallow roasting pan. Roast in 425° oven for 50 to 60 minutes or till meat thermometer *nearly* registers 130°. Remove meat; cool 20 minutes. Reserve pan drippings. Trim any fat from roast.

Meanwhile, in mixing bowl stir together flour and salt. Cut in shortening till mixture resembles small peas. Gradually add cold water, a tablespoon at a time, tossing with fork till mixture is dampened. Form into ball. Roll out, on lightly floured surface, to a 14x12-inch rectangle. Spread pastry with Mushroom Filling to within 1 inch on all sides.

Place meat, top side down, into center of pastry. Draw up long sides to overlap. Brush with a little egg to seal. Trim ends; fold up and brush with a little more egg to seal. Place roast on lightly greased baking sheet, seam side down. Brush egg over all. Reroll pastry trimmings. Cut strips; place on roast. Brush with remaining egg. Bake in 425° oven for 30 to 35 minutes or till golden. Prepare Gravy. Serve with roast. Serves 12.

Mushroom Filling: In small skillet cook 8 ounces *fresh mushrooms,* chopped (3 cups), and 1 large *leek,* chopped (½ cup), in 2 tablespoons *butter or margarine* about 6 minutes or till tender. Remove from heat. Stir in ¼ cup *fine dry bread crumbs,* 3 tablespoons of the reserved marinade (save remaining marinade for gravy), and ½ cup *liver pâté* or one 4¾-ounce can *liver spread.* Cover and chill filling at least 1 hour.

Gravy: Heat ¾ cup *water* with reserved pan drippings till any solids are dissolved. Blend together 3 tablespoons all-purpose *flour* and ½ cup *cold water*; add to pan drippings along with ¼ cup of the reserved marinade. Cook and stir till thickened and bubbly. Season with salt and pepper.

SAUCY MEATBALL PLATTER

Serve over hot cooked spaghetti–

2 beaten eggs
1½ cups soft bread crumbs
½ cup chopped onion
¾ cup milk
2 tablespoons snipped parsley
½ teaspoon dried oregano, crushed
1½ pounds ground beef
2 tablespoons cooking oil
1 11-ounce can condensed cheddar cheese soup
2 tablespoons all-purpose flour
⅓ cup dry white wine

In large bowl combine eggs, bread crumbs, onion, ¼ *cup* of the milk, the parsley, oregano, ½ teaspoon *salt,* and dash *pepper.* Add beef; mix well. Shape into 30 meatballs. In large skillet brown half the meatballs at a time in hot oil. Drain off excess fat. Return all meatballs to skillet. Stir together soup and flour; gradually add remaining ½ cup milk. Pour over meatballs in skillet. Cover; simmer 10 to 12 minutes. Stir in wine. Cover; simmer 5 minutes. Serve over spaghetti. Serves 6.

SPINACH BEEF ROLL

A budget-stretching dish for company

2 tablespoons all-purpose flour
½ teaspoon salt
¼ teaspoon garlic salt
⅛ teaspoon pepper
1 2-pound piece beef round steak, cut ¾ inch thick

. . .

½ of a 10-ounce package frozen chopped spinach, cooked and well drained (½ cup)
¾ cup soft bread crumbs (1 slice bread)
⅓ cup grated parmesan cheese
2 tablespoons finely chopped onion
¼ teaspoon ground sage
¼ teaspoon dried thyme, crushed
2 tablespoons shortening
⅔ cup dry red wine

Combine flour, salt, garlic salt, and pepper; pound into round steak till meat is about ¼ inch thick. Cut meat in half lengthwise. Combine spinach, bread crumbs, cheese, onion, sage, and thyme; spread over both pieces of meat. Roll up each piece jelly-roll fashion, starting from shorter side. Skewer or tie each meat roll to secure.

In skillet brown meat slowly on all sides in hot shortening. Transfer to 12 x 7½ x 2-inch baking dish. Pour wine over meat. Cover. Bake in 350° oven for 45 minutes. Uncover; bake 15 minutes more or till tender. To serve, pass juices with meat. Makes 8 servings.

*For your next dinner party, select one of these three elegant entrées—*Boeuf en Croute, Crab-stuffed Chicken *(recipe on page 80),* or Sensational Veal Stew *(recipe on page 82). Trim the main dishes with parsley or watercress sprigs.*

STEAK STRIP PLATTER

Meat and vegetables arranged on a platter and served with wine sauce—

½ cup dry white wine
¼ cup cooking oil
1 pound beef flank steak, bias cut in very thin bite-size strips
4 ounces whole fresh mushrooms
1 small onion, sliced
3 tablespoons chopped green onion
1 clove garlic, minced
¼ cup butter *or* margarine
¾ cup beef broth
⅓ cup dry white wine
¼ teaspoon salt
2 tablespoons cornstarch
1 cup light cream
2 10-ounce packages frozen broccoli spears
1 15-ounce can sliced potatoes
   Garlic salt

Combine ½ cup wine and the cooking oil; pour over meat in shallow dish. Cover; marinate at room temperature 2 hours, stirring occasionally. Drain meat well and set aside.

In medium skillet cook mushrooms, onion, green onion, and garlic in butter or margarine till vegetables are tender but not brown. Add the beef broth, ⅓ cup wine, and salt. Combine cornstarch and cream. Add to broth mixture. Cook and stir till mixture is thickened and bubbly. Remove to bowl; keep warm.

Meanwhile, cook broccoli spears according to package directions; drain and keep warm. Heat potatoes in separate saucepan.

In hot skillet over high heat, cook drained meat quickly about 1½ minutes; sprinkle generously with garlic salt. Arrange broccoli, potatoes, and meat on serving platter. Spoon sauce mixture over top. Makes 4 servings.

TERIYAKI BEEF-RICE RING

Meat loaf with an Oriental flair—

½ cup long grain rice
1 cup water
¼ teaspoon salt
1 10-ounce package frozen Chinese-style vegetables with sauce cubes
¼ cup water
2 tablespoons snipped parsley
1 tablespoon butter *or* margarine, softened
   . . .
1 slightly beaten egg
¼ cup dry sherry
3 tablespoons soy sauce
1 cup soft bread crumbs (1½ slices bread)
½ cup chopped onion
¼ teaspoon celery salt
   Dash pepper
1½ pounds lean ground beef
   Fresh *or* frozen pea pods, stir-fried
   Cherry tomatoes, halved
   Bottled teriyaki sauce

In small saucepan combine uncooked rice, the 1 cup water, and the salt. Bring to boiling. Reduce heat and simmer, covered, *just* 15 minutes. Meanwhile, in another saucepan combine Chinese vegetables and the ¼ cup water. Cook and stir just till sauce cubes are melted. Remove from heat.

Combine the cooked rice, Chinese vegetables, parsley, and butter or margarine; set aside.

In mixing bowl combine egg, sherry, soy, bread crumbs, onion, celery salt, and pepper. Add beef; mix well. Pack rice-vegetable mixture tightly into bottom of 5½-cup ring mold. Pat meat mixture atop. Unmold onto 15x10x1-inch baking pan. Cover loosely with foil. Bake in 350° oven for 1 hour. Using two wide spatulas, carefully transfer ring to serving platter. Fill center of ring with stir-fried pea pods and halved cherry tomatoes. Pass teriyaki sauce. Makes 6 servings.

CHICKEN-SAUSAGE TERRINE

Serve as the entrée for a supper or luncheon, or as a picnic main dish—

8 slices bacon
2 cups cubed cooked chicken
½ small onion, cut up
½ clove garlic, minced
1 beaten egg
⅓ cup dry red wine
1 cup soft bread crumbs
¾ teaspoon salt
¼ teaspoon pepper
¼ teaspoon dried thyme, crushed
¼ teaspoon dried marjoram, crushed
1 pound bulk pork sausage
8 ounces thinly sliced boiled ham

Lay bacon into shallow baking pan. Bake in 350° oven for 10 minutes; turn once. Lay bacon crosswise in a 9x5x3-inch loaf pan.

Grind chicken, onion, and garlic through fine blade of food chopper. Combine egg, wine, bread crumbs, salt, pepper, thyme, and marjoram. Add chicken mixture and sausage; mix well. Pat a *third* of the ground meat mixture over bacon in loaf pan. Cover with *half* the ham. Repeat layers, ending with ground meat.

Cover loosely with foil. Place another pan of the same size filled with dry beans atop loaf. Seal edges of foil to edges of loaf pan. Bake in 350° oven 1¼ to 1½ hours. Cool. Remove from pan. Wrap tightly; chill at least 8 hours. Slice to serve. Makes 8 to 10 servings.

Chill Chicken-Sausage Terrine *before slicing to serve. Trim the platter with greens and cherry tomatoes, and garnish the bacon-encased meat loaf with parsley, if desired.*

LAMB WITH TARRAGON SAUCE

Chops with an elegant-tasting sauce—

4   lamb shoulder chops, cut ¾ inch thick
2   tablespoons cooking oil
    Salt
    Pepper
1   cup chicken broth
⅓   cup dry white wine
1½ teaspoons dried tarragon, crushed

. . .

4   teaspoons cornstarch
2   tablespoons cold water
1   3-ounce can sliced mushrooms, drained
½   cup dairy sour cream

In large skillet brown chops in hot oil. Season with salt and pepper. Add chicken broth, wine, and tarragon. Cover and simmer 40 to 45 minutes or till tender. Remove chops; keep warm. Skim excess fat from drippings.

Combine cornstarch and water. Stir cornstarch mixture along with mushrooms into hot mixture. Cook and stir till thickened and bubbly. Stir about *half* of the hot mixture into sour cream. Return all to skillet. Heat through but *do not boil.* Serve sauce over chops. Serves 4.

WINED SHORT RIBS

Beef ribs grilled over slow coals—

½ cup water
½ cup dry red wine
1   teaspoon dried thyme, crushed
½   teaspoon garlic salt
½   teaspoon lemon pepper
2   pounds beef short ribs

In Dutch oven mix water, wine, thyme, garlic salt, and lemon pepper. Add ribs. Cover; simmer 1¼ to 1½ hours. Drain, reserving liquid. Grill over *slow* coals 15 to 20 minutes. Turn often; brush on the reserved liquid. Makes 4 servings.

MEATBALLS WITH SPAETZLE

Wine and caraway flavor the sauce—

1   beaten egg
¼   cup milk
¼   cup fine dry bread crumbs
1   tablespoon snipped parsley
½   teaspoon salt
¼   teaspoon poultry seasoning
    Dash pepper
1   pound ground beef

. . .

1   cup dry white wine
¾   cup water
1   4-ounce can chopped mushrooms
¾   cup chopped onion
1½ teaspoons instant beef bouillon granules
1   cup dairy sour cream
4   teaspoons all-purpose flour
½   to 1 teaspoon caraway seed
    Spaetzle

In bowl combine egg, milk, crumbs, parsley, salt, poultry seasoning, and pepper. Add meat and mix well. Shape mixture into twenty-four 1½-inch meatballs.

In skillet brown meatballs; drain off excess fat. Stir in wine, water, *undrained* mushrooms, onion, and bouillon granules. Cover and simmer 30 minutes. Remove meatballs; keep warm.

Combine sour cream, flour, and caraway seed. Stir into the wine mixture. Cook and stir till mixture thickens and bubbles. Arrange meatballs and sauce over Spaetzle. If desired, sprinkle with snipped parsley. Makes 4 to 6 servings.

Spaetzle: In bowl combine 2 cups all-purpose *flour* and 1 teaspoon *salt*. Add 2 beaten *eggs* and 1 cup *milk*; beat well. Let stand 5 to 10 minutes. Place batter in coarse-sieved colander (with ¼-inch holes). Hold over large kettle of rapidly boiling salted water. Press batter through colander with back of wooden spoon or rubber spatula. Cook and stir 5 minutes; drain.

MUSHROOM-SPINACH PASTA

For late-supper dining—

2   cups cream-style cottage cheese (16 ounces)
2   3-ounce packages cream cheese, softened
½   cup finely chopped onion
2   tablespoons butter *or* margarine

. . .

1   *or* 2 3-ounce cans chopped mushrooms, drained
⅓   cup dry white wine
½   teaspoon dried thyme, crushed
¼   teaspoon salt
    Dash pepper
1   5⅓-ounce can (⅔ cup) evaporated milk
1   10-ounce package frozen chopped spinach, cooked and well drained
10 ounces spaghetti, cooked and drained
    Grated parmesan cheese (optional)

With an electric mixer beat cottage cheese and cream cheese together till nearly smooth. In a saucepan cook onion in butter or margarine till tender but not brown. Add mushrooms, wine, thyme, salt, and pepper. Stir in cheese mixture, evaporated milk, and drained spinach. Heat through.

Gently toss the cheese mixture with the hot cooked spaghetti. Pass parmesan cheese, if desired. Makes 6 servings.

Three main dishes that are easy on the budget yet special enough for guests include Meatballs with Spaetzle, Salmon-Broccoli Crepes (recipe on page 89), and Mushroom-Spinach Pasta.

CHICKEN PAPRIKASH

Use Hungarian or regular paprika—

1 2½- to 3-pound broiler-fryer chicken, cut up
2 tablespoons cooking oil
1 cup chopped onion
1 tablespoon paprika
¼ cup dry white wine
¼ cup *condensed* chicken broth
½ cup dairy sour cream
  Hungarian Gnocchi

In large skillet brown chicken in hot oil on all sides; season with salt and pepper. Remove chicken. Add onion to skillet; cook till tender. Stir in paprika. Return chicken to pan, turning once to coat with paprika mixture. Add wine and broth. Bring to boiling. Reduce heat; cover and simmer 30 to 35 minutes or till tender. Remove chicken; keep warm.

Boil skillet drippings about 2 minutes or till reduced to ½ cup. Stir in sour cream; heat through but *do not boil.* Pour sauce over chicken. Serve over Hungarian Gnocchi. Sprinkle with additional paprika and garnish with snipped parsley, if desired. Serves 4.

Hungarian Gnocchi: In large heavy saucepan combine 1⅓ cups *water,* ½ cup *unsalted butter,* ¾ teaspoon *salt,* and several dashes *cayenne.* Bring to boiling, stirring to melt butter. Add 1⅓ cups all-purpose *flour* all at once; stir with wooden spoon till dough comes away from sides of pan and forms smooth ball. Remove from heat. Stir in 4 teaspoons *dijon-style mustard.* Add 3 *eggs,* one at a time, beating well after each. Set aside.

In 4-quart saucepan heat 12 cups *water* and 1 tablespoon *salt* to boiling; reduce heat till water barely simmers. Fit pastry bag with a large plain tip (No. 8). Fill bag with dough. Pipe out 1-inch-long pieces of dough, cutting with knife and letting pieces drop into simmering water. Cover pan, leaving lid slightly ajar. Simmer *gently* for 15 minutes. Remove with slotted spoon.

CHICKEN WITH WINE

Red wine and tomato puree are used in the sauce for chicken pieces—

1 medium onion, chopped (½ cup)
2 tablespoons snipped parsley
1 clove garlic, minced
½ teaspoon dried marjoram, crushed
¼ cup butter *or* margarine

. . .

1 2½-pound broiler-fryer chicken, cut up
⅓ cup tomato puree
⅓ cup dry red wine
½ teaspoon salt
⅛ teaspoon pepper

. . .

2 teaspoons cornstarch
1 tablespoon cold water

In heavy skillet cook onion, parsley, garlic, and marjoram in *half* of the butter or margarine for 5 minutes (do not brown). Remove vegetables from pan and set aside. Add remaining butter to skillet; brown chicken on all sides (brown half the chicken at a time, if necessary). Combine the tomato puree, wine, salt, and pepper. Add to skillet along with the cooked vegetables.

Cover and simmer for 45 minutes. Remove chicken to a serving platter. Spoon off excess fat from sauce. Combine cornstarch and the cold water; add to sauce in skillet. Cook and stir till thickened and bubbly. Pour over chicken. Garnish with parsley, if desired. Makes 4 servings.

CRAB-STUFFED CHICKEN

Pictured on page 75—

4 whole large chicken breasts (12 ounces each), halved, skinned, and boned
3 tablespoons butter
¼ cup all-purpose flour
¾ cup milk
¾ cup chicken broth
⅓ cup dry white wine
¼ cup chopped onion
1 tablespoon butter
1 7½-ounce can crab meat, drained, flaked, and cartilage removed
1 3-ounce can chopped mushrooms, drained
½ cup coarsely crumbled saltine crackers (10 crackers)
2 tablespoons snipped parsley
½ teaspoon salt
  Dash pepper
1 cup shredded process Swiss cheese (4 ounces)
½ teaspoon paprika

Place one chicken piece, boned side up, between two pieces of waxed paper. Working from center out, pound chicken lightly with meat mallet to make cutlet about ⅛ inch thick (8x5-inch rectangle). Repeat with remaining chicken. Set chicken aside.

In saucepan melt the 3 tablespoons butter; blend in flour. Add milk, chicken broth, and wine all at once. Cook and stir till mixture thickens and bubbles. Set aside.

In skillet cook onion in the 1 tablespoon butter till tender but not brown. Stir in the crab, mushrooms, cracker crumbs, parsley, salt, and pepper. Stir in *2 tablespoons* of the wine mixture. Top each chicken piece with about ¼ cup crab mixture. Fold sides in; roll up. Place seam side down into 12x7½x2-inch baking dish. Pour remaining wine mixture over. Bake, covered, in 350° oven for 1 hour or till chicken is tender. Uncover; sprinkle with cheese and paprika. Bake 2 minutes longer or till cheese melts. Makes 8 servings.

COQ AU VIN

Use a burgundy to make this—

4   ounces salt pork, diced
1   pound small boiling onions, peeled (16)
5   ounces fresh whole mushrooms
2   cloves garlic, halved
2   2½-pound broiler-fryer chickens, cut up
5   tablespoons all-purpose flour
1⅔ cups dry red wine
1   cup chicken broth
2   tablespoons snipped parsley
½   teaspoon dried thyme, crushed
2   bay leaves
3   tablespoons butter *or* margarine, softened

In 8-quart Dutch oven cook salt pork till crisp and browned; remove from pan, reserving ¼ cup drippings (if necessary, add cooking oil to drippings to make ¼ cup). Cook onions, mushrooms, and garlic in drippings for 5 minutes; remove from pan and set aside. Add *half* the chicken pieces to remaining drippings; brown thoroughly on all sides. Remove from Dutch oven. Repeat with remaining chicken. Blend *2 tablespoons* of the flour, ¾ teaspoon *salt*, and ¼ teaspoon *pepper* into drippings in pan. Add wine, broth, parsley, thyme, and bay leaves. Return chicken, onions, mushrooms, and salt pork to pan. Simmer, covered, about 40 minutes or till chicken is tender. Remove chicken from sauce; discard bay leaves. Spoon off excess fat.

Blend the remaining 3 tablespoons flour and the butter to a smooth paste. Using a wire whisk, stir into the hot sauce in pan. Cook and stir till bubbly. Season with salt and pepper. Return chicken to pan; heat through.

To serve, arrange chicken on serving plate; top with sauce. Sprinkle with additional snipped parsley, if desired. Serve with thin toasted French bread slices, if desired. Makes 6 to 8 servings.

WINE AND WILD RICE BAKE

Use either cooked chicken or turkey—

1   6-ounce package long grain and wild rice mix
½   cup chopped onion
½   cup chopped celery
2   tablespoons butter *or* margarine
1   10¾-ounce can condensed cream of mushroom soup
½   cup dairy sour cream
⅓   cup dry white wine
½   teaspoon curry powder
2   cups cubed cooked chicken *or* turkey
¼   cup snipped parsley

Prepare rice mix according to package directions. Meanwhile, in saucepan cook onion and celery in butter or margarine till tender but not brown. Blend in soup, sour cream, wine, and curry powder. Stir in chicken or turkey and cooked rice. Turn mixture into a 12x7½x2-inch baking dish. Bake, uncovered, in 350° oven for 35 to 40 minutes. Stir before serving. Garnish with parsley. Serves 4 to 6.

Microwave Cooking Directions: Prepare rice mix atop range according to package directions. Meanwhile, place onion, celery, and butter or margarine into a 2-quart nonmetal casserole. Cook, covered, on high power in a countertop microwave oven 2 to 2½ minutes or till tender.

Blend in soup, sour cream, wine, and curry powder. Stir in chicken or turkey and cooked rice. Micro-cook, covered, 8 to 10 minutes or till heated through, giving casserole a half turn after 5 minutes. Garnish with parsley.

CURRY-WINE SAUCED CHICKEN

Garnish with paprika and parsley—

½   cup dry white wine
1   teaspoon instant chicken bouillon granules
1   clove garlic, minced
1   teaspoon curry powder
½   teaspoon seasoned salt
3   whole chicken breasts, split
2   teaspoons cornstarch
1   3-ounce can sliced mushrooms, drained

In large skillet combine wine, bouillon granules, garlic, curry, seasoned salt, 1 cup *water*, and ¼ teaspoon *pepper*. Bring to boiling. Add chicken; reduce heat. Cover and simmer 25 to 30 minutes or till tender. Remove chicken and place on platter. Combine cornstarch and 2 tablespoons *cold water*; slowly stir into pan juices. Cook and stir over low heat till bubbly. Stir in mushrooms. Pour over chicken. Serves 6.

CHICKEN TERIYAKI

Part of the cooking is done ahead—

⅓   cup soy sauce
⅓   cup dry sherry
2   tablespoons sugar
½   teaspoon ground ginger
6   chicken drumsticks
6   chicken thighs

In large kettle combine first 4 ingredients and 1¼ cups *water*; bring to boiling. Add chicken. Cover; simmer about 30 minutes or till tender. Remove chicken from soy mixture. Cool chicken and liquid separately. Place chicken into bowl; pour soy mixture over. Cover; chill at least 4 hours or overnight. (Soy mixture will gel.)

Preheat broiler. Remove fat from soy mixture. Remove chicken; place on rack in broiler pan. Heat soy mixture. Broil chicken 3 inches from heat about 10 minutes; turn often and brush each side once with sauce. Pass sauce. Serves 6.

SENSATIONAL VEAL STEW

Pictured on page 75–

2 to 2½ pounds boneless veal, cut into 1-inch cubes
6 tablespoons butter *or* margarine
1 pound small boiling onions, peeled (16)
12 ounces fresh mushrooms, sliced (4½ cups)
1 clove garlic, minced
1 teaspoon salt
⅛ teaspoon freshly ground pepper
⅓ cup all-purpose flour
1 10¾-ounce can condensed chicken broth
¾ cup dry white wine
1 carrot, halved
1 leek, sliced
1 stalk celery, halved
2 sprigs parsley
¼ teaspoon dried thyme
1 bay leaf
3 tablespoons lemon juice
2 egg yolks
¾ cup whipping cream
  Grated nutmeg
  Lemon wedges

In a Dutch oven or large saucepan simmer veal in butter or margarine over low heat, uncovered, about 10 minutes (do not brown). Add onions, mushrooms, garlic, salt, and pepper; cook, uncovered, 10 minutes more. Sprinkle flour over meat; stir till blended. Add broth, wine, carrot, leek, and celery.

Place parsley, thyme, and bay leaf into cheesecloth bag, and tie. Add to mixture. Cover and simmer, stirring occasionally, for 30 minutes or till meat is tender. Remove and discard cheesecloth bag, carrot, and celery. Stir in lemon juice.

Beat together egg yolks and the cream. Stir about *1 cup* of the hot mixture into the egg yolk mixture; return all to hot mixture, stirring constantly. Heat till mixture is bubbly and slightly thickened. Transfer to serving bowl; sprinkle with nutmeg. Serve with lemon wedges. Makes 6 to 8 servings.

SAUSAGE AND SAVOY CABBAGE

If you like, substitute green cabbage for the savoy cabbage–

2 pounds link Italian sausage
2 cups dry red wine
1 clove garlic, minced
  . . .
½ cup finely chopped onion
2 tablespoons finely chopped salt pork
1 16-ounce can stewed tomatoes, cut up
1 cup water
1 medium head savoy cabbage, coarsely chopped
  Salt
  Pepper

Using fork, prick sausage casing several times. Cut sausage into 3-inch pieces. Place sausage into large mixing bowl. Add wine and minced garlic. Set sausage aside to marinate for 30 minutes.

Drain sausage pieces, reserving marinade. In large saucepan or Dutch oven, cook sausage, onion, and salt pork till meats are browned and onion is tender. Add the reserved wine marinade. Cover and simmer for 20 minutes.

Stir in the *undrained* tomatoes, water, and cabbage. Cover and simmer 20 minutes more, stirring occasionally. Season to taste with salt and pepper. To serve, ladle into individual soup bowls. Serve with crusty Italian bread, if desired. Makes 8 to 10 servings.

VENISON STEW

If venison isn't available, substitute beef stew meat–

1 pound boneless venison *or* beef stew meat, cut into ½-inch cubes
1½ cups water
1 teaspoon salt
⅛ teaspoon coarsely ground pepper
  . . .
½ cup dry red wine
4 medium carrots, cut into thirds
2 medium potatoes, peeled and cubed (1½ cups)
1 cup fresh *or* frozen cranberries
½ cup chopped onion
1 stalk celery, cut into julienne strips
1 clove garlic, minced
2 tablespoons sugar
2 tablespoons worcestershire sauce
1½ teaspoons Hungarian *or* regular paprika
3 juniper berries (optional)
2 whole cloves
1 bay leaf
  . . .
½ cup cold water
¼ cup rye flour
  Cooked wild rice

In 3-quart saucepan combine venison, the 1½ cups water, salt, and pepper. Bring to boiling; reduce heat. Cover and simmer 1¼ hours.

Stir in wine, carrots, potatoes, cranberries, onion, celery, garlic, sugar, worcestershire, paprika, juniper berries, cloves, and bay leaf. Cover and simmer 45 minutes or till vegetables are tender.

Combine cold water and flour; stir into stew. Cook and stir till thickened and bubbly. Serve with wild rice. Makes 4 servings.

ESTOFADO

Serve this stew over hot rice—

1   pound beef stew meat, cut into 1-inch cubes
1   tablespoon cooking oil
1   cup dry red wine
1   7½-ounce can tomatoes, cut up
1   large onion, sliced ¼ inch thick
1   green pepper, cut into strips
¼   cup raisins
¼   cup dried apricots, halved
1   clove garlic, minced
1½ teaspoons salt
⅛   teaspoon pepper
     . . .
1   teaspoon dried basil
1   teaspoon dried thyme
1   teaspoon dried tarragon
1   bay leaf
     . . .
½   cup sliced fresh mushrooms
¼   cup sliced ripe olives
1   cup cold water
1   tablespoon all-purpose flour
     Hot cooked rice

In large skillet brown meat in hot oil. Add wine, *undrained* tomatoes, onion, green pepper, raisins, apricots, garlic, salt, and pepper. Place basil, thyme, tarragon, and bay leaf into cheesecloth bag, and tie. Add to mixture. Simmer, covered, 1 hour.

Add mushrooms and olives; simmer 30 minutes more. Remove and discard cheesecloth bag. Combine cold water and flour; stir into stew. Cook and stir till mixture thickens and bubbles. Serve over hot cooked rice. Makes 6 servings.

BEEF AND BEAN RAGOUT

Starts with dry kidney beans—

1   cup dry, dark red kidney beans
3   cups water
¼   cup all-purpose flour
½   teaspoon salt
2   pounds beef stew meat, cut into 1-inch cubes
2   tablespoons cooking oil
1   16-ounce can tomatoes, cut up
¾   cup dry red wine
1½ teaspoons salt
1   teaspoon sugar
2   cloves garlic, minced
½   teaspoon dried thyme, crushed
⅛   teaspoon pepper
1   bay leaf
     . . .
3   potatoes, peeled and cubed (3 cups)
2   medium onions, cut into wedges
½   cup chopped green pepper

Rinse beans. Place into 3-quart saucepan with the 3 cups water; soak overnight. (Or bring to boiling; reduce heat and simmer 2 minutes. Remove from heat; cover and let stand 1 hour.) *Do not drain.*

Bring beans to boiling; reduce heat. Cover and simmer 45 minutes. Drain. Combine flour and the ½ teaspoon salt; coat stew meat with the flour mixture.

In 4-quart Dutch oven brown *half* the meat at a time in hot oil. To all the meat add drained beans, the *undrained* tomatoes, wine, 1½ teaspoons salt, the sugar, garlic, thyme, pepper, and bay leaf. Bring to boiling. Reduce heat. Cover and simmer 1 to 1¼ hours or till meat is nearly tender. Add potatoes, onions, and green pepper. Cook 30 minutes more or till meat and potatoes are tender. Remove bay leaf before serving. Serves 8 to 10.

OXTAIL VEGETABLE SOUP

Serve this entrée in soup plates—

2   pounds oxtails, cut into 1½-inch lengths
3   tablespoons all-purpose flour
2   tablespoons cooking oil
1   medium onion, chopped (½ cup)
1   16-ounce can tomatoes, cut up
1   10½-ounce can condensed beef broth
½   cup water
½   cup dry red wine
1   teaspoon sugar
½   teaspoon salt
½   teaspoon dried thyme, crushed
¼   teaspoon pepper
1   bay leaf
     . . .
4   medium carrots, peeled and cut into julienne strips (2 cups)
4   medium parsnips, peeled and cut into julienne strips (2 cups)
½   cup frozen peas

Trim fat from oxtails. Coat oxtails with the flour. In Dutch oven brown meat in hot oil. Add onion, *undrained* tomatoes, beef broth, water, wine, sugar, salt, thyme, pepper, and bay leaf. Bring mixture to boiling. Reduce heat; cover and simmer 2 hours or till meat is just tender. Skim off excess fat. Add the carrot strips and parsnip strips; cover and simmer 25 minutes longer. Add peas; cook 5 minutes more. Serve in soup plates. Makes 4 servings.

CIOPPINO

Fish stew seasoned with herbs—

1 pound fresh *or* frozen fish
  fillets
½ large green pepper, cut into
  ½-inch squares
2 tablespoons finely chopped
  onion
1 clove garlic, minced
1 tablespoon cooking oil
  . . .
1 16-ounce can tomatoes, cut
  up
1 8-ounce can tomato sauce
½ cup dry white *or* red wine
3 tablespoons snipped parsley
½ teaspoon salt
¼ teaspoon dried oregano,
  crushed
¼ teaspoon dried basil, crushed
  Dash pepper
2 4½-ounce cans shrimp,
  drained and deveined, *or* 1
  12-ounce package frozen
  shelled shrimp
1 7½-ounce can minced clams

Thaw fish, if frozen. Remove skin
from fillets and cut fillets into
1-inch pieces; set aside.

In 3-quart saucepan cook green
pepper, onion, and garlic in oil till
onion is tender but not brown. Add
undrained tomatoes, tomato sauce,
wine, parsley, salt, oregano, basil,
and pepper. Bring to boiling. Reduce heat; cover and simmer 20
minutes.

Add fish pieces, shrimp, and *undrained* clams to tomato mixture.
Bring just to boiling. Reduce heat;
cover and simmer 5 to 7 minutes or
till fish and shrimp are done. Makes
6 servings.

*Fish fillets, shrimp, and clams go
into the making for herb-seasoned
Cioppino. Use fresh or frozen fillets
and canned or frozen shrimp to
prepare this stew.*

SKIP JACK CHOWDER

An oyster stew flavored with wine—

2 medium red onions, chopped
¼ cup snipped parsley
2 tablespoons butter
1 tablespoon soy sauce
1 teaspoon dried thyme,
  crushed
1 bay leaf
  Dash bottled hot pepper
  sauce
1 pint fresh oysters
2 cups milk
½ cup light cream
2 cups shredded American
  cheese (8 ounces)
½ cup dry white wine

In large saucepan cook onion and
parsley in butter till tender but not
brown. Stir in soy, thyme, bay leaf,
pepper sauce, and ½ teaspoon *salt*.
Add oysters; cook and stir over low
heat about 5 minutes or just till
edges curl. Stir in milk and cream.
Heat through. Add cheese, stirring
till melted. Remove from heat; stir
in wine. Makes 6 servings.

SCALLOP-WINE SOUP

Topped with cheese and parsley—

1 pound fresh *or* frozen
  scallops, thawed
1 large onion
2 tablespoons butter
¼ cup all-purpose flour
3½ cups milk
1 4-ounce can mushroom
  stems and pieces, drained
½ cup dry white wine
½ cup shredded Swiss cheese
1 tablespoon snipped parsley

Halve large scallops. Cut onion into
thin wedges. Cook onion in butter,
covered, over low heat 15 minutes
or till tender; stir occasionally. Stir
in flour. Add milk; cook and stir
over medium-high heat till bubbly.
Add mushrooms, scallops, 1 teaspoon *salt*, and dash *pepper*. Cover;
simmer 5 minutes. Stir in wine;
heat. Top with cheese and parsley.
Serves 6.

FISH-WINE CHOWDER

Choose from suggested fish fillets—

1 pound fresh *or* frozen brook
  trout *or* pike fillets
1 pound fresh *or* frozen
  halibut *or* haddock fillets
6 slices bacon
  . . .
1 medium onion, chopped (½
  cup)
2 shallots, chopped (1
  tablespoon)
1½ cups dry white wine
1½ cups water
1 teaspoon salt
¼ teaspoon dried thyme,
  crushed
1 stalk celery, quartered
2 cloves garlic, halved
4 sprigs parsley
2 whole cloves
  . . .
3 tablespoons all-purpose flour
3 tablespoons butter *or*
  margarine, softened
¼ cup light cream

Thaw fish, if frozen; cut fish into
bite-size pieces. Cook bacon in
4½-quart Dutch oven; drain, reserving 2 tablespoons drippings.
Crumble bacon; set aside.

Cook onion and shallots in reserved bacon drippings till tender.
Remove from heat. Add wine, water, salt, and thyme. To make a
bouquet garni, place celery, garlic,
parsley, and whole cloves into
cheesecloth, and tie. Add to pan.

Bring to boiling. Reduce heat;
cover and simmer for 20 minutes.
Remove cheesecloth bag. Add fish
to Dutch oven. Cover and cook
gently 8 to 10 minutes or till fish
flakes when tested with fork.

Blend flour and softened butter
or margarine to a smooth paste; stir
into simmering liquid. Stir in
cream. Cook and stir till thickened
and bubbly. Return bacon to pan.
Season to taste. Serves 8.

SEAFOOD THERMIDOR

*Cod replaces the lobster in this famil-
iar seafood dish–*

1 pound fresh *or* frozen cod
   fillets
1 small onion, quartered
   Lemon slice
   . . .
1 10¾-ounce can condensed
   cream of shrimp soup
3 tablespoons all-purpose flour
¼ cup milk
¼ cup dry white wine
¼ cup shredded mozzarella
   cheese (1 ounce)
2 tablespoons snipped parsley
   . . .
½ cup soft bread crumbs
2 tablespoons grated parmesan
   cheese
2 teaspoons butter *or*
   margarine
½ teaspoon paprika

Thaw fish, if frozen. Remove skin,
if necessary. Cut fish into ½-inch
cubes. Place fish, onion, and lemon
into greased skillet. Add water to
cover. Bring to boiling; reduce
heat. Cover and simmer 5 to 6 minutes or till fish flakes easily with a
fork.

Meanwhile, in small saucepan
blend soup and flour; gradually stir
in milk and wine. Cook and stir till
thickened and bubbly. Stir in the
mozzarella and parsley. Heat
through. Carefully drain fish well;
fold into sauce. Spoon into 4
coquille shells.

Combine bread crumbs, parmesan cheese, butter, and paprika.
Sprinkle over sauce. Broil 1 to 2
minutes. Makes 4 servings.

*For a special supper entrée, serve
Coquilles Florentine, a seafood
mixture of shrimp and scallops, plus
fresh mushrooms and spinach. The
sauce is flavored with wine and
Swiss and parmesan cheese.*

COQUILLES FLORENTINE

*Pernod, an optional ingredient,
is an anise-flavored liqueur–*

8 ounces fresh mushrooms
1 tablespoon chopped shallots
¾ cup fish stock *or* clam juice
½ cup dry white wine
8 ounces fresh *or* frozen large
   shrimp in shells
8 ounces fresh *or* frozen
   scallops
2 teaspoons chopped shallots
2 tablespoons butter
2 tablespoons butter
2 tablespoons all-purpose flour
¾ cup milk
1 slightly beaten egg yolk
1½ cups chopped fresh spinach,
   cooked and well drained
2 tablespoons shredded Swiss
   cheese
2 tablespoons grated
   parmesan cheese
1 tablespoon Pernod (optional)
1 cup soft bread crumbs
1 tablespoon butter, melted

Remove stems from mushrooms;
slice mushroom caps and set aside.
In saucepan combine mushroom
stems, 1 tablespoon shallots, fish
stock or clam juice, and wine. Bring
to boiling. Reduce heat; simmer,
covered, 5 minutes. Add shrimp;
simmer 3 minutes. Add scallops;
simmer 5 minutes more. Remove
shrimp and scallops. Strain remaining liquid and return to saucepan;
bring to boiling. Boil gently till liquid is reduced to ¾ cup. Set aside.

Cook sliced mushroom caps and
2 teaspoons shallots, covered, in 2
tablespoons butter for 5 minutes.
Shell and clean shrimp; split
lengthwise and cut halves into
¾-inch pieces. Slice scallops ¼
inch thick. Combine shrimp, scallops, and sliced mushrooms.

In saucepan melt 2 tablespoons
butter; stir in flour. Cook and stir
over medium heat 2 minutes. Add
reduced fish stock and milk; cook
and stir till thickened.

Gradually stir about *half* the mixture into egg yolk. Return all to
saucepan. Cook and stir 2 minutes
more. Add spinach, cheeses, and
Pernod; stir to melt cheese. Stir
into shrimp mixture. Spoon into 6
large or 12 small coquille shells or
ramekins.

Combine bread crumbs and 1
tablespoon melted butter. Sprinkle
crumbs atop shells. Bake in 400°
oven 10 to 15 minutes. Serves 6.

OYSTERS LAFITTE

Six oyster shells make one serving–

¼ cup butter *or* margarine
2 cups chopped fresh
   mushrooms
1 cup chopped cooked shrimp
¼ cup chopped green onion
¼ cup snipped parsley
1 clove garlic, minced
24 fresh oysters, shucked, *or* 2
   8-ounce cans oysters
½ cup dry white wine
½ teaspoon salt
   Dash cayenne
1 cup light cream
¼ cup all-purpose flour
   Rock salt
⅓ cup fine dry bread crumbs
2 tablespoons butter, melted
⅛ teaspoon paprika

In skillet melt the ¼ cup butter.
Add mushrooms, shrimp, onion,
parsley, and garlic. Cook 1 minute.
Drain oysters, reserving liquid (add
water if needed to make ¾ cup).
Add oyster liquid, wine, salt, and
cayenne to skillet. Bring to boiling;
reduce heat and simmer for 1 minute. Combine cream and flour. Stir
into wine mixture; cook and stir till
thickened and bubbly. Arrange 24
oyster shells on bed of rock salt in
shallow baking pan. Place 1 oyster
into each shell; spoon about 2 tablespoons sauce over each oyster.
Combine bread crumbs, melted
butter, and paprika. Sprinkle over
mixture in shells. Bake in 450° oven
for 10 to 12 minutes or till heated
through. Makes 4 servings.

HALIBUT VERONIQUE

Poached fish with a grape-wine sauce—

4 fresh *or* frozen halibut steaks
   (about 1½ pounds)
      · · ·
¾ cup cold water
½ cup dry white wine
5 teaspoons cornstarch
1 tablespoon chopped green
   onion
2 teaspoons instant chicken
   bouillon granules
      · · ·
1 cup green grapes, halved and
   seeded
1 tablespoon snipped parsley
1 tablespoon butter *or*
   margarine
1 teaspoon lemon juice

Thaw fish, if frozen. Place halibut steaks in greased skillet. Add water to cover. Bring to boiling; reduce heat. Cover and simmer for 8 to 10 minutes or till fish flakes easily when tested with a fork. Remove halibut and place on platter; keep warm.

Meanwhile, in small saucepan combine cold water, wine, and cornstarch; add green onion and bouillon granules. Cook and stir till thickened and bubbly. Add grapes, parsley, butter or margarine, and lemon juice; heat through. To serve, spoon sauce over fish. Garnish fish with lemon wedges and parsley sprigs, if desired. Makes 4 servings.

HADDOCK PROVENCALE

Fish fillets with a tomato sauce—

6 fresh *or* frozen haddock fillets
   (1½ pounds)
   Salt
   Paprika
      · · ·
¼ chopped onion
1 clove garlic, minced
1 tablespoon butter *or*
   margarine
½ cup dry white wine
2 tomatoes, peeled, seeded, and
   coarsely chopped, *or* 1
   16-ounce can tomatoes,
   drained and cut up
1 3-ounce can chopped
   mushrooms, drained
2 tablespoons snipped parsley
1 vegetable bouillon cube
1 teaspoon sugar
¼ cup cold water
2 teaspoons cornstarch

Thaw fillets, if frozen. Sprinkle each fillet with salt and paprika. Roll up fillets; secure with wooden picks.

Cook onion and garlic in butter or margarine till onion is tender but not brown. Add wine. Stir in tomatoes, mushrooms, snipped parsley, bouillon cube, and sugar; bring to boiling.

Add fish; reduce heat. Cover and simmer for 15 to 20 minutes or till fish flakes easily. Remove fish and place on platter; remove wooden picks. Keep warm.

Combine cold water and cornstarch. Add to tomato liquid in skillet. Cook and stir till mixture thickens and bubbles. Spoon sauce over fish. Garnish with additional snipped parsley, if desired. Makes 6 servings.

HADDOCK NEWBURG

Served in baked patty shells—

1 pound fresh *or* frozen
   haddock fillets
6 tablespoons butter *or*
   margarine
2 tablespoons all-purpose flour
1⅔ cups light cream
3 beaten egg yolks
⅓ cup dry white wine
1 2-ounce jar (¼ cup) sliced
   pimiento, chopped
1 tablespoon lemon juice
½ teaspoon salt
   Dash white pepper
4 frozen patty shells, baked

Thaw fish, if frozen. Place fish in greased skillet. Add salted water to cover. Bring to boiling; reduce heat. Cover and simmer, for 5 to 10 minutes or till fish flakes easily with a fork. Drain fish; break into large chunks. Set fish aside.

In saucepan melt butter or margarine; blend in flour. Add light cream all at once. Cook and stir over medium heat till mixture thickens and bubbles. Stir about *half* of the hot mixture into egg yolks; return all to hot mixture. Cook, stirring constantly, till thickened.

Gently stir in fish chunks, wine, pimiento, lemon juice, salt, and pepper. Heat through. Serve mixture in patty shells. Garnish with leaf lettuce and cherry tomatoes, if desired. Makes 4 servings.

STUFFED FLOUNDER ROLLS

Fish with a deviled egg filling

4   fresh *or* frozen flounder fillets (about 1 pound)
    Salt
    Pepper

      . . .

3   hard-cooked eggs, chopped
2   tablespoons snipped parsley
2   tablespoons mayonnaise *or* salad dressing
1½ teaspoons dijon-style mustard

      . . .

1   10-ounce package frozen chopped broccoli, thawed
2   cups cooked long grain rice
1   10¾-ounce can condensed cream of shrimp soup
½   cup dry white wine

Thaw fillets, if frozen. Sprinkle each fillet with salt and pepper. Combine chopped egg, parsley, mayonnaise, and mustard. Spoon 3 to 4 table-spoons of the egg mixture atop each fillet; roll up lengthwise. If neces-sary, secure with wooden picks.

Combine broccoli and rice. In bowl stir together soup and the wine. Stir *1 cup* of the soup mixture into rice mixture. Turn rice mixture into a 1½-quart round au gratin dish or 10x6x2-inch baking dish. Place fish rolls atop rice. Pour re-maining soup mixture over fish rolls. Cover with foil. Bake in 375° oven for 25 minutes. Uncover. Bake 20 to 25 minutes more or till fish flakes easily when tested with a fork. Remove wooden picks. Makes 4 servings.

SALMON-BROCCOLI CREPES

Pictured on page 79—

2   beaten eggs
1½ cups milk
1   tablespoon butter, melted
1   cup all-purpose flour
¼   cup butter *or* margarine
¼   cup chopped onion
¼   cup all-purpose flour
1¾ cups milk
2   cups shredded American cheese
⅓   cup dry white wine
1   10-ounce package frozen chopped broccoli
1   7¾-ounce can salmon, drained, boned, and flaked

Combine eggs, 1½ cups milk, and 1 tablespoon melted butter. Add 1 cup flour; beat with rotary beater till smooth. Lightly grease a 6-inch skillet; heat.

Pour 2 tablespoons batter into hot skillet. Lift pan and tilt from side to side till batter covers bot-tom. Return to heat. Cook about 2 minutes or till bottom of crepe is lightly browned and top appears dry. Turn out onto paper toweling. Repeat, making 12 crepes in all. Stack crepes with two sheets of waxed paper between crepes; set aside.

In saucepan melt ¼ cup butter. Add onion and cook till tender but not brown. Stir in the ¼ cup flour and ¼ teaspoon *salt*. Add the 1¾ cups milk. Cook and stir till mixture thickens and bubbles. Add cheese, stirring till melted. Stir in wine. Remove from heat; set aside.

For filling, cook broccoli accord-ing to package directions; drain. Chop any large pieces. Fold in sal-mon and ¾ *cup* of the sauce. Spoon about 3 tablespoons filling onto un-browned side of each crepe. Roll up jelly-roll fashion. Arrange, seam side down, in 12x7½x2-inch baking dish. Bake, covered, in 375° oven for 15 to 20 minutes. To serve, heat remaining sauce and pour over crepes. Makes 4 servings.

SCALLOP-BROCCOLI STIR-FRY

Use a wok or skillet for cooking—

1   12-ounce package fresh *or* frozen scallops
2   tablespoons cold water
2   teaspoons cornstarch
½   cup dry sherry
1   teaspoon sugar
1   teaspoon instant beef bouillon granules
¼   teaspoon salt

      . . .

1   8-ounce can bamboo shoots, drained
1   medium onion, sliced
1   6-ounce can whole mushrooms, drained
1   tablespoon cooking oil

      . . .

1   10-ounce package frozen broccoli spears, thawed and halved crosswise

Thaw scallops, if frozen. Stir to-gether the cold water and cornstarch; stir in sherry, sugar, bouillon granules, and salt. In wok or large skillet stir-fry bamboo shoots, onion, and mushrooms in hot oil till onion is crisp-tender. Remove from wok; keep warm. Add broccoli to wok. Stir-fry 2 minutes. Push broccoli up sides of wok; add scallops to center of wok. Stir-fry on high heat for 3 minutes. Return vegetables to wok; stir sherry mixture and pour over all. Cook and stir till mixture is bubbly. Season to taste with salt and pep-per. Makes 3 or 4 servings.

HOLIDAY BREAD PUDDING

Strawberries, cinnamon, and white wine flavor the sauce—

2   slightly beaten eggs
2¼ cups milk
½   cup packed brown sugar
1   teaspoon vanilla
¼   teaspoon salt
5   slices day-old, firm-
      textured white bread, cut
      into 1-inch cubes
⅓   cup raisins

. . .

1   10-ounce package frozen
      strawberries, thawed
2   tablespoons cold water
1   tablespoon cornstarch
¼   teaspoon ground cinnamon
½   cup dry white wine
      Several drops red food
      coloring (optional)

In a bowl combine eggs, milk, brown sugar, vanilla, and salt. Stir in the bread cubes and raisins. Let stand 5 minutes. Pour mixture into an 8x1½-inch round baking dish. Place dish into large shallow pan on oven rack. Pour hot water into larger pan to depth of 1 inch. Bake in 350° oven about 50 minutes or till a knife inserted off-center comes out clean.

Meanwhile, for sauce sieve the strawberries. In saucepan combine the cold water, cornstarch, and cinnamon. Stir in the sieved berries. Cook and stir till thickened and bubbly. Stir in the wine and several drops of red food coloring, if desired. Heat through.

Serve warm bread pudding with the strawberry-wine sauce. Makes 6 servings.

SHERRIED RASPBERRY TARTS

Tart shells are made with small crepes. Freeze remaining crepes to use another time—

12   Mini Crepes
2   10-ounce packages frozen
      red raspberries
¼   cup sugar
¼   cup cornstarch
½   cup cream sherry
      Whipped cream

Prepare Mini Crepes. Thaw the raspberries; drain, reserving 1 cup syrup. Reserve 12 whole berries for garnish; set aside.

In small saucepan combine the sugar and cornstarch; stir in the reserved raspberry syrup and cream sherry. Cook and stir till thickened and bubbly. Stir in the drained raspberries.

Fit the mini crepes, browned side up, into small shallow dessert dishes or custard cups. Spoon a scant 3 tablespoons filling into each crepe shell. Ruffle edges with fingers; chill till filling is firm. Garnish with a little whipped cream and the reserved whole raspberries. Makes 12 tarts.

Mini Crepes: In small mixer bowl beat together 3 *egg yolks* and ¼ teaspoon *vanilla.* Stir in 3 tablespoons melted *butter or margarine.* Stir together ½ cup all-purpose *flour* and ¼ cup *sugar.* Add to egg yolk mixture alternately with ½ cup *milk,* beating after each addition.

In large mixer bowl beat 3 *egg whites* till stiff peaks form (tips stand straight). Gently fold batter mixture into whites.

Brush a 6-inch skillet with *cooking oil*; heat. Spoon a rounded tablespoonful batter into pan. Spread with back of spoon into a 4-inch circle. Cook over medium-high heat for 45 to 60 seconds or till underside is browned. Loosen with metal spatula; invert onto paper toweling. Repeat with remaining batter to make 24 crepes.

STRAWBERRY-RICE PARFAITS

A special rice pudding mixture—

1¼ cups milk
⅔   cup quick-cooking rice
¼   cup sugar
½   teaspoon salt
1   teaspoon vanilla

. . .

2   cups strawberries, halved
½   cup water
¼   cup sugar
4   teaspoons cornstarch
¼   cup cream sherry
½   cup whipping cream
½   cup toasted chopped
      almonds

In medium saucepan combine the milk, *uncooked* rice, ¼ cup sugar, and salt. Bring to boiling. Reduce heat and simmer, uncovered, for 10 minutes, stirring occasionally. Remove from heat; stir in vanilla. Cover and let stand 5 minutes. Chill.

In saucepan crush *1 cup* of the berries; stir in the water. Bring to boiling; boil 2 minutes. Sieve. Combine the remaining ¼ cup sugar and the cornstarch. Stir into strawberry mixture. Return to saucepan. Cook and stir till thickened and bubbly. Cool slightly. Stir in the cream sherry. Cover and chill.

Whip cream; fold into rice mixture. Fold remaining berries into the sherry mixture.

Spoon *half* the berry mixture into 6 parfait glasses. Top with *half* the almonds and *half* the rice mixture. Repeat the layers with berry mixture, almonds, and rice mixture. Makes 6 servings.

CONFECTIONERS' CONCEIT

Chill the glass container for this dessert in the refrigerator section, not in the freezer—

1   pint lime sherbet
1   pint orange sherbet
1   pint raspberry sherbet
1   pint pineapple sherbet

. . .

1   10-ounce package frozen red raspberries
1½ cups cranberry juice cocktail
¾   cup sugar
3   tablespoons cornstarch
½   cup dry red wine

. . .

1   11-ounce can mandarin orange sections, drained
    Blueberries
    Strawberries, halved
    Red raspberries

Scoop sherbet into balls and place on waxed paper or foil-lined baking sheet. Freeze till very hard.

In saucepan bring raspberries and cranberry juice to boiling. Press through sieve. Return juice mixture to saucepan. Stir together the sugar and cornstarch. Add to sieved raspberry mixture. Cook and stir till thickened and bubbly. Stir in the wine. Cool thoroughly.

Carefully arrange the frozen sherbet balls and each of the fruits alternately in a large chilled brandy snifter or a large chilled glass bowl. Serve sherbet and fruit in individual dishes with the raspberry-wine sauce. Makes 12 servings.

STRAWBERRY TRIFLE

Uses about ¾'s of a 10-inch cake—

½   cup granulated sugar
2   tablespoons cornstarch
1   16-ounce package frozen strawberries, thawed
1   tablespoon lemon juice
2   eggs
1   egg yolk
1¾ cups milk
8   cups cubed sponge cake
¾   cup cream sherry
1   egg white
1   tablespoon sifted powdered sugar
1   cup whipping cream
¼   teaspoon vanilla
¼   cup slivered almonds

In saucepan combine ¼ *cup* of the granulated sugar and the cornstarch. Add berries with syrup. Cook and stir over medium heat about 10 minutes or till thick and bubbly. Stir in lemon juice. Cover surface with waxed paper. Cool.

In heavy saucepan combine eggs, egg yolk, milk, remaining ¼ *cup* granulated sugar. Cook and stir about 10 minutes or till it coats a metal spoon. Remove from heat. Pour into medium bowl; set inside larger bowl filled with ice. Stir 1 to 2 minutes to hasten cooling.

Place 3 *cups* of the cake cubes into a 2-quart serving dish. Sprinkle with ¼ *cup* sherry. Reserve ¼ cup strawberry mixture for garnish. Top cake cubes with *half* the remaining strawberry mixture and *half* the custard. Repeat layers, using another 3 cups cake cubes, ¼ cup sherry, remaining strawberry mixture, and remaining custard. Add remaining cake cubes; sprinkle with remaining sherry.

Beat egg white to soft peaks. Add powdered sugar; beat to stiff peaks. Whip cream and vanilla to soft peaks; fold into egg white. Spread mixture atop cake cubes. Refrigerate 6 hours or overnight. Before serving, dot with reserved strawberry mixture and sprinkle with nuts. Makes 10 to 12 servings.

GRAPE CHANTILLY PIE

A frozen pie with a special topper—

    Vanilla Wafer Crust
⅓   cup cream sherry
1   package fluffy white frosting mix (for 2-layer cake)
1   cup small curd cream-style cottage cheese
1   cup dairy sour cream
¼   cup grape jelly
1   tablespoon cream sherry
1   cup red grapes, halved, seeded, and drained

Prepare Vanilla Wafer Crust. Chill about 1 hour or till firm.

Add enough water to the ⅓ cup cream sherry to measure ½ cup liquid. In saucepan heat the ½ cup liquid till boiling. Pour hot liquid over frosting mix in mixer bowl; beat 7 minutes at high speed of electric mixer.

Place cottage cheese and sour cream in blender container. Cover and blend till smooth. Pour mixture into a bowl; fold in frosting mixture. Turn cottage cheese-frosting mixture into wafer crust. Freeze pie several hours or overnight till firm.

Shortly before serving, combine grape jelly and the 1 tablespoon cream sherry in small saucepan. Cook and stir till boiling; boil 1 minute more. Remove from heat; cool to lukewarm. Just before serving, remove pie from freezer. Arrange grape halves on top of pie. Glaze grapes with jelly mixture. Slice pie and serve immediately.

Vanilla Wafer Crust: In mixing bowl combine 1½ cups finely crushed *vanilla wafers* (36 wafers) and 6 tablespoons melted *butter or margarine*. Turn crumb mixture into a 9-inch pie plate. Spread the crumb mixture evenly in the pie plate. Press onto bottom and sides to form a firm, even crust. Chill.

Where to Seek More Information

The *Wine Institute*, 165 Post Street, San Francisco, CA 94108 is an excellent source for material on California wines. Most of the state's wineries are members, and the Institute is active in publicizing new developments in wine making.

"California's Wine Wonderland," a free touring guide to California wineries, is available from the Wine Institute. A "Wine Study Course" is also free. Write the Wine Institute at the above address for an application form.

The *American Wine Society* represents most Eastern and Midwestern wineries and is a source of various publications on technical aspects of grape growing and wine making. Its address is 4218 Rosewold Ave., Royal Oak, MI 48073.

Like the Wine Institute, the American Wine Society is a nonprofit association, but it is more loosely structured, with chapters scattered throughout the country. These chapters have meetings and wine tastings on their own, which are often reported in the *American Wine Society Journal,* a quarterly publication you receive with annual membership dues of $12.50, from the Michigan address listed above.

Les Amis du Vin (Friends of Wine) is a national association of chapters—usually operated through retail wine shops—that meet for tastings, dinners, and lectures on wine. An excellent bimonthly magazine, *Friends of Wine,* sells for nine dollars a year. Address: Les Amis du Vin, 2302 Perkins Place, Silver Spring, MD 20910.

Winery Newsletters

Write to any of these addresses if you would like to be on the winery's mailing list. These newsletters often describe how specific wines are made, which new wines have proved successful, and what trends the winemaster sees for the future.

Buena Vista Winery, "The Grapevine," P.O. Box 182, Sonoma, CA 95476.

Concannon Vineyard, "Vineyard Vignettes," P.O. Box 432, Livermore, CA 95452.

Geyser Peak Winery, "News from the Peak," 4340 Redwood Highway, Suite 220, San Rafael, CA 94903.

Guild Wineries and Distilleries, "Winemasters' News," 500 Sansome St., San Francisco, CA 94111.

Inglenook Vineyards, "Inglenook Notes," P.O. Box 19, Rutherford, CA 94573.

Hanns Kornell Champagne Cellars, "Hanns Kornell Champagne Newsletter," Box 249, St. Helena, CA 94574.

Charles Krug Winery, "Bottles and Bins," P.O. Box 191, St. Helena, CA 94574.

Mirassou Vineyards, "Latest Press," Rt. 3, Box 344, San Jose, CA 95121.

The Monterey Vineyard, "Winemaker Notes," Box 780, Gonzales, CA 93926.

Papagni Vineyards, "Papagni Press," 31754 Ave. 9, Madera, CA 93637.

Sebastiani Vineyards, Inc. (unnamed, but a very good one) P.O. Box AA, 389 Fourth St. E, Sonoma, CA 95476.

Ste. Michelle Vintners, "The Woodinville Press," P.O. Box 1976, Woodinville, WA 98072.

Many American wineries will send you small recipe booklets that feature ways to use wine in cooking. Two Eastern sources of such material are the Taylor Wine Company of Hammondsport, N.Y. 14840, and Gold Seal Vineyards, Executive Offices, Empire State Building, New York, N.Y. 10001.

Wine Country Touring

Most of the large wineries schedule tours and tastings during the week, sometimes daily, all year. They may actually demonstrate how wine is made there or show it to you on films. Some permit picnicking on the grounds and will sell cheese or sandwiches to eat with a bottle of their wine. A few have restaurants in conjunction with the winery.

Small wineries should not be visited without an appointment. Some have no time for visitors—the family may do all the work themselves, and it is hard, ceaseless work!

Actually, you may find that *touring* wineries is harder work than you expected. There's a lot to see and do at many of them, and the tasting room often is the final stop on a lengthy guided tour. So don't plan to visit too many wineries in the same day. And during harvest season and all year on weekends, be prepared for substantial crowds.

The Wine Institute's touring guide and several of the books on our list will help identify California wineries that can be visited. In addition, there are three privately published California wine touring booklets: "Napa Valley Wine Tour," "Central Coast Wine Tour," and "Sonoma Mendocino Wine Tour." Each of these may be obtained for $5.95 from Vintage Image, 1335 Main St., St. Helena, CA 94574.

For visiting New York's wineries, there is an excellent small guide: "New York State Wines and Champagnes and Guide to Wineries," available for 25 cents from New York State Dept. of Agriculture and Markets, Bldg. 8, State Campus, Albany, N.Y. 12235.

Glossary

Acid, Acidic: A sharp or tart taste in a wine, not necessarily indicating spoilage. All wines contain some acid; too little may leave the flavor flat or dull. Often, a young wine has a somewhat acid taste that diminishes or disappears during aging.

Aging: Extra time in cask or bottle improves most red wines and a few white wines. Many fine wines are aged two years in oak barrels and another year in the bottle before they are sold. White wines that require aging usually need only a few months; a white wine that is several years old may actually have deteriorated in quality.

Aperitif Wine: One meant to be served before a meal as an appetizer.

Aroma: The smell of the grape variety that carries over into the wine. It is most perceptible in Concord and Muscat grapes.

Astringent: A sharp, puckery taste in a new wine due to tannin (see that listing). Aging in cask or bottle is the remedy.

Balanced: Harmonious blending of all the elements of taste in a wine. There should be neither too much nor too little acid, tannin, and sugar. The quality of the grapes and the skill of the winemaster have much to do with achieving this subtle result.

Big Wine: One having strong flavor and full body, to serve with flavorsome food.

Blanc de Blancs: White wine made from white grapes; this French phrase usually refers to sparkling wine made from fine Chardonnay grapes. A few table wines also carry this name.

Blending: Mixing different batches of the same wine (or different varieties of wine) in order to improve quality. One batch may have too much acid, for example; another, too little. A blending of the two often can create just the right balance of acidity.

Body: The viscosity or "feeling" of a wine in the mouth—which is related in part to its alcohol content. A wine may have a thin, medium, full, or heavy body.

Botrytis: *Botrytis cinerea* is the "noble rot," a beneficial mold that shrivels ripe grapes at harvesttime, concentrating their juices. The wine made from them is rich and luscious—and usually expensive.

Bouquet: A combination of wine odors—that of the grape variety (see "Aroma"), plus others that develop in the wine during fermentation and aging in oak.

Breathe, Breathing: Allowing air to reach a wine by uncorking or pouring it. The wine breathes to shed any unpleasant odors, such as sulfur, and to take in oxygen, which may bring out the bouquet.

Brut: Dry or lacking sweetness, used in reference to sparkling wines. This is the driest type of champagne normally sold; see also "Extra Dry."

Charmat Process: A shortcut way of producing sparkling wines by fermenting them in large vats instead of in bottles. Named for its inventor, this process is common for inexpensive champagnes; the label tells you if the Charmat process has been used.

Cross: See "Hybrid."

Dessert Wine: A term formerly used to indicate sweet wines, such as sherries, ports, and muscatels, that are fortified with brandy to bring them up to an alcohol content of around 16 to 18 percent. (See "Fortified.") Now, the meaning is more precise: a wine to be served with desserts or by itself after a meal. Dessert wines today include such sweet wines as Muscat Canelli and "late harvest" White Riesling, which have alcohol contents as low as just 10 to 12½ percent.

Dry Wine: One lacking sweetness, with most or all of its sugar converted into alcohol by fermentation. Most table wines are dry or fairly dry—to complement the flavors of most foods prior to the dessert course.

Extra Dry: Term used on a label to indicate that a sparkling wine is slightly sweet (contradictory but true!). See also "Brut" and "Sec."

Fermentation: The process of converting the natural sugars in a wine into alcohol. Yeasts are introduced into tanks of *must* (see that listing) to start the process; it stops when the sugars are depleted or when the alcohol level reaches about 13 percent and kills the yeast. Secondary fermentation takes place in the bottle (or in bulk—see "Charmat process") in sparkling wines and gives them their distinctive fizz.

Finish: The aftertaste of wine. Some wines taste sweet at first but "finish" dry in the mouth. Any wine taste that leaves the palate quickly is said to have a "short" finish. A taste that lingers carries a "long" finish—a quality to be desired.

Flat: Usually said of wine lacking in acidity (see "Acid").

Flavored Wine: "Pop" wines are often flavored with citrus or other fruit. Vermouth is flavored with herbs and spices. Only natural flavors may be added to a wine under Federal regulations.

Flowery: A floral smell in wines such as Gewurztraminer and young wines made of White Riesling grapes.

Fortified: Wine in which fermentation was stopped and the alcohol content increased by the addition of grape brandy. This process is used for sherries, ports, and other wines whose alcohol content reaches 16 to 18 percent—sometimes even more in very sweet wines.

Foxy: Term used to describe the strong grapey smell and taste of some wines made from our native Eastern grapes, such as Concord, Catawba, Niagara, and Delaware. Such grapes once were called "fox grapes," which accounts for the word "foxy."

Fruit Wine: Wine made of fruit *other than* grapes, such as cherries, various berries, apples, or peaches. See detailed listing on page 25.

Full, Full-bodied: Wine causing a sensation of fullness in the mouth (see "Body").

Generic: In the United States, our generic wines borrow European names which have specific meanings in their own countries but not here. Examples include burgundy, chablis, rhine wine, and sauterne. Many wineries are phasing out such labels in favor of more descriptive and accurate names (see "Varietal"). However, it's likely that burgundy (for an inexpensive red wine) and chablis (for an inexpensive white) will be in use in America for quite some time.

Hybrid: A new grape variety produced from two different species of grapes—for improved resistance to disease, better adaptation to climate, or higher quality wine. Technically, a "cross" involves two kinds of grapes from within one species; for example, Ruby Cabernet results from a cross between Cabernet Sauvignon and Carignane, both members of the *vitis vinifera* species. The new hybrid Seyval Blanc was developed from mixed parentage of *vitis vinifera* (European) and *vitis labrusca* (American) grapes.

Labrusca: Native Eastern American grape family including the Concord, Catawba, Niagara, and Delaware. They are known for strong aromas and flavors (see "Foxy").

Late Harvest: A wine made from grapes picked after their juices are extra sweet and concentrated (see "Botrytis").

Must: The crushed grapes and their juice before the fermentation process begins.

Musty: A cellar-like smell that usually dissipates when the wine is allowed to "breathe" (see that listing).

Nose: Term frequently used in place of "smell" or "aroma," as in "The nose of this wine is very flowery."

Nutty: Having a nutlike smell or taste; often said of sherry.

Peppery: A spicy nose and flavor in red wine.

Proprietary Wine: One carrying a name originated by a specific winery—essentially a brand name. Examples include Paul Masson's "Emerald Dry," Gallo's "Tyrolia," and Christian Brothers' "Chateau LaSalle."

Sec: A French word meaning "dry"; however, when applied to champagne it has come to indicate a medium sweet one (see "Extra Dry").

Stemmy: Tasting of grape stems and leaves. Proper care at the winery should avoid this.

Still Wine: Any non-sparkling wine.

Sulfury: A smell of sulfur that doesn't immediately disperse when the bottle is opened. Some sulfur is needed to preserve a wine, but it should never be present in excess. If noticeable after a few moments of breathing, the wine is bad.

Table Wine: Red, white, or pink wines of 11 to 13 percent alcohol, suitable for serving with food.

Tannic, Tannin: A substance in grape skins, seeds, and stems necessary for the development of fine red wines. In young wines, it is unpleasant, but the "puckery" taste disappears in time and a harmonious blending of wine characteristics takes place. See "Astringent" and "Balanced."

Varietal: Term used to indicate that a wine is made predominantly of the grape variety named on the label. For example, Zinfandel wine is supposed to be made from Zinfandel grapes. A new Federal law now specifies that a minimum of 75 percent of a varietal wine be made from the grape listed on the label.

Vintage Wine: Wine from a single year named on the label, rather than a blend from several years. Vintage wines are not necessarily good; there are fine years, average years, and poor years for most wines.

General Index

Recipe Index